200 curries

D0755617

hamlyn | **all colour cookbook**

200 curries

Sunil Vijayakar

An Hachette Livre UK Company
www.hachettelivre.co.uk

First published in Great Britain in 2008 by
Hamlyn, a division of Octopus Publishing Group Ltd,
2–4 Heron Quays, London E14 4JP
www.octopusbooks.co.uk

ISBN: 978-0-600-61728-0

A CIP catalogue record of this book is available from the
British Librar.

Printed and bound in China

10 9 8 7 6 5 4 3 2

People with known nut allergies should avoid recipes
containing nuts or nut derivatives, and vulnerable people
should avoid dishes containing raw or lightly cooked eggs.

Ovens should be preheated to the specific temperature. If
using a fan-assisted oven, follow the manufacturer's
instructions for adjusting the time and temperature. Grills
should also be preheated.

Both metric and imperial measurements are given for
the recipes. Use one set of measurements only,
not a mixture of both.

Standard level spoon measurements are used in all recipes.
1 tablespoon = one 15 ml spoon
1 teaspoon = one 5 ml spoon

Fresh herbs should be used unless otherwise stated.

Medium eggs should be used unless otherwise stated.

Some of the recipes in this book have previously appeared in
other titles published by Hamlyn including:
30-minute Indian by Sunil Vijayakar
Delicious Food for Diabetes by Louise Blair
M&S Fab Fast Food
Vegetarian Thai by Jackum Brown

Contents

introduction

introduction

The word 'curry' is thought to derive from the South Indian Tamil word *kari*. It is generally used to describe any spiced, saucy dish, best known in Indian, Sri Lankan, Bangladeshi, Indonesian, Malaysian, Burmese (Myanmar), Thai and other South Asian and Southeast Asian cuisines.

The concept of curry was first brought to the West by British colonists in India in the 18th century. Civil servants and officers in the British Raj acquired a taste for spicy dishes and brought their new-found recipes home to Britain or to other parts of the Empire, and adapted them to suit their own tastes. Mulligatawny Soup (see page 30), for example, is a mild anglicized version of a fiery South Indian sauce.

The most common misconception is that a curry is a hot and spicy dish. Of course some curries are extremely hot, but on the whole most recipes are a balanced blend of spices and herbs with a delicate and highly sophisticated flavour.

curries today

We now know and love curries that come from different countries around the world. They differ greatly in their taste and content, with vast regional variations and many well-defined cuisines, each with its own history.

Whatever its origins, a curry usually contains a selection of fresh and dried herbs and spices. Depending on the dish, other ingredients could include chillies, curry leaves, ginger, garlic, shallots, lemon grass, coconut milk, palm sugar, tamarind paste, Thai fish sauce, shrimp paste and chopped tomatoes – the list goes on. The recipes and ingredients vary from region to region, as well as from country to country.

As knowledgeable and passionate food lovers today, we have embraced curries from all over the world. You can buy most of the ingredients in any large supermarket, and with the miracle of Internet shopping you can even order exotic ingredients and have them delivered to your door.

This book offers exciting recipes to suit every palate, and you may soon join the ranks of the millions of curry addicts around the world.

dry spices and other ingredients

The following ingredients will be useful in your quest to create wonderful curries. The flavour of dry spices decreases with time, so buy them in small quantities and use them up quickly so you always have a fresh supply.

amchoor

Dried mango powder, used as a souring agent in Indian curries. Substitute with a little lemon juice or tamarind paste if unavailable.

asafoetida

Also known as 'devil's dung', this plant resin is found in lump or ground form, and is very strong in flavour. Usually used in very tiny amounts in lentil preparations, it is believed to counteract flatulence.

cardamom

This spice is usually used whole in its pod, as an aromatic to flavour rice and curries. You can also use the little black seeds inside the pods, by crushing them and using as part of a spice mixture.

cassia

Also known as Chinese cinnamon, cassia has a coarser texture and stronger flavour than cinnamon.

chilli

Whole dried red chillies add fiery heat to a curry; dried chilli flakes tend to have a milder flavour. Chilli powders made from dried chillies vary in heat from mild to very hot.

cinnamon

This sweet and warming aromatic spice comes from the bark of a tree and is available as sticks or rolled bark. Also widely used in ground form.

cloves

Native to Indonesia, the clove is an aromatic dried bud from an evergreen tree. Used whole or ground, it has a penetrating and sweet flavour.

coconut milk & cream

Coconut milk and cream is widely available in cans or cartons. They are added to curries to impart a rich, creamy texture. You can make your own coconut milk by mixing the grated flesh of fresh coconut with water. Blend well, then sieve to remove the coconut flesh.

coriander

The small, pale brown seeds of the coriander plant are available whole or ground, and form the base of many curry pastes and mixes. They have a tangy flavour, similar to lemon.

cumin
Essential in Asian cooking, these small brown elongated seeds are used whole or ground, and have a distinctive warm, pungent aroma. Whole seeds may be dry-roasted and sprinkled over a dish just before serving.

dhana-jeera
This is a mixture of equal quantities of ground coriander and ground cumin.

fennel seeds
These small, pale green seeds have a subtle aniseed flavour and are used as a flavouring in some spice mixtures.

fenugreek seeds
These tiny seeds are usually square in shape and are shiny yellow in colour. They are used widely in pickles and ground into spice mixes.

garam masala
This classic spice mix is usually added to a dish at the end of the cooking time so the flavours stay fresh. It usually comprises ground cardamom, cloves, cumin, cinnamon, peppercorns and nutmeg.

gram flour
Also known as *besan*, this pale yellow flour is made from dried chickpeas, and is used for thickening and binding. It is the main ingredient in savoury batters.

ground bean sauce
Widely available in Oriental and Asian stores, this sauce is a mixture of soy beans, flour, sugar, salt and water.

kecap asin and kecap manis
Kecap asin is a thick, dark soy sauce and kecap manis is a sweeter version. Both are made from salted, fermented soya beans.

mustard seeds
Black, brown or yellow, these tiny round seeds are widely used as a flavouring, and are usually fried in oil until they pop to impart a mellow, nutty flavour.

nigella seeds
Also known as black onion seeds or *kalonji*, these tiny black, oval seeds are most frequently used to flavour breads and pickles.

palm sugar
Known as *jaggery* in India and *nam tan peep* in Thailand, this is the sugar produced from the sap of palms. Sold in cakes or cans, the sugar has a deep caramel flavour and light brown colour. It is used in curries to balance the spices.

saffron

These deep orange strands are the dried stamens from a special crocus and are used to impart a musky fragrance and golden colour to rice dishes and desserts.

sambal oelek

This is a spicy chilli and garlic paste used in the cooking of Indonesia and the Straits and as a condiment to be eaten with rice.

shrimp paste

Also known as *kapee*, this is a pungent preserve, made from pounding shrimp with salt and leaving it to decompose. It is sold in small jars and has a very powerful aroma that disappears when cooked.

star anise

Star-shaped and dark brown in colour, this spice has a decidedly anise flavour. It is used widely in Indian cooking.

sweet chilli sauce

This a sweet and mild sauce made from red chillies, sugar, garlic and vinegar.

tamarind paste

Used as a souring agent in curries, the paste from the tamarind pod is widely available and can be used straight from the jar. You can also buy it in semi-dried pulp form, which needs to be soaked in warm water and strained before use.

Thai fish sauce

Also widely known as *nam pla*, this sauce is one of the main ingredients in Thai cooking and is made from the liquid extracted from salted, fermented fish.

turmeric

This bright orange-yellow rhizome has a warm, musky flavour and is used in small quantities to flavour lentil and rice dishes and curries. It is widely available as a dried, ground powder.

urad dhal

Although it is a type of lentil, this round white pulse is used as a spice when it is fried to release and intensify its nutty flavour.

white poppy seeds

Also known as *khus*, these tiny white poppy seeds are used in Indian cooking, mainly to thicken sauces and curries.

fresh aromatics & spices

The following fresh herbs and aromatics, including Thai basil, lemon grass, lime leaves, coriander and curry leaves, and 'wet' spices, such as onion, ginger, galangal, garlic and shallots, are essential when cooking various different curries.

chillies

Fresh green and red chillies are used in many curries to give heat and flavour. Much of the heat resides in the pith and seeds, so if you want the chilli flavour with less heat, slit the chillies in half and remove the pith and seeds.

coriander

It is usually the delicate coriander leaves that are used to flavour dishes, but the stalks and roots are also used.

curry leaves

These highly aromatic leaves are used fresh in Indian and Southeast Asian cooking. The leaves freeze very well and can be used straight from the freezer.

galangal

Just like its cousin ginger, this rhizome is used in curries and other savoury dishes. It is peeled and cut into very fine slivers or chopped very finely before use. You can substitute ginger if you don't have any.

garlic

One of the essential flavours used in cooking curries, garlic is used with ginger and onion as the base for many dishes. It is used sliced, crushed or grated.

ginger

Another indispensable aromatic, fresh root ginger is peeled before use. It has a fresh, peppery flavour and is used in both savoury and sweet preparations.

lemon grass

Known as *sere* in Indonesia, *serai* in Malaysia, *takrai* in Thailand and *tanglad* in the Philippines, this green grass is used for its citrus flavour and aroma. It can be used whole by bruising the base of the stalk to release the flavour, or it can be finely sliced or chopped.

lime leaves

These leaves come from the knobbly kaffir lime plant and are highly aromatic. They are usually finely shredded, but can be left whole. They freeze well and can be used straight from the freezer.

onions

This humble vegetable forms the base of many curries and similar dishes. Used sliced or chopped, it is usually fried slowly before the other curry ingredients are added.

shallots

These small sweet and pungent members of the onion family are widely used in Southeast Asian cooking. The easiest way to peel them is to slice them in half first.

Thai basil

Found in Oriental greengrocers, this delicate herb is usually used to garnish and flavour a curry. You can substitute regular basil if you cannot find any.

homemade curry powder & pastes

There is a huge variety of really good-quality, commercial curry powders and pastes from which to choose. Curry powders are usually labelled mild, medium or hot, but there are more specific mixes, including tandoori spice mix and Madras curry powder. Equally, there is a wide variety of pastes available.

While ready-made curry powders and pastes do save time, nothing can compare to the aromatic flavour and explosion of taste that a homemade curry powder or paste can bring to a dish. See page 72 for a homemade Thai green curry paste recipe and page 78 for a homemade Thai red curry paste recipe. There are also a number of recipes that use curry powder. You could make your own curry powder using the following recipe. The number of chillis you use will ultimately determine the heat of your curry powder.

basic curry powder

Makes 10 tablespoons

4 tablespoons **coriander seeds**
2 tablespoons **cumin seeds**
4 teaspoons **black peppercorns**
3 teaspoons **brown mustard seeds**
2 teaspoons **fenugreek seeds**
5–6 **cloves**
5–6 dried **red chillies**, crumbled
1–2 teaspoons ground **turmeric**

Place all the ingredients, except for the turmeric, in a dry heavy-based frying pan and place over a medium heat. Stir and dry roast for 2–3 minutes or until the spices emit a light and fragrant aroma. Add the turmeric and stir for 10–15 seconds. Remove from the heat and allow to cool. Transfer to a clean coffee grinder and blend until smooth. Store in an airtight container.

starters

crispy spiced egg salad

Serves **4**

Preparation time **20 minutes**

Cooking time **15 minutes**

sunflower oil, for deep frying

6 large **eggs**, boiled for
  4 minutes and shelled

75 g (3 oz) **palm sugar**

6 tablespoons **tamarind juice**

5 tablespoons **Thai fish
  sauce**

2 tablespoons **water**

2 tablespoons **sweet chilli
  sauce**

6 **shallots**, thinly sliced

4 **garlic** cloves, thinly sliced

2 **red chillies**, deseeded and
  thinly sliced

100 g (3½ oz) mixed **salad
  leaves**

small handful of fresh
  coriander leaves

25 g (1 oz) **bean sprouts**

sunflower oil, for frying

Pour sunflower oil into a wok until one-third full and heat to 180–190°C (350–375°F), or until a cube of bread browns in 30 seconds. Place the eggs in a slotted spoon, in batches, and carefully lower into the hot oil. Deep fry for 2–3 minutes or until lightly golden. Remove, drain on kitchen paper and keep warm.

Place the palm sugar, tamarind juice, fish sauce and measured water in a small pan and heat until the sugar dissolves, then simmer gently for 3–4 minutes. Transfer to a bowl and stir in the sweet chilli sauce.

Meanwhile, place 2 tablespoons of the oil in a nonstick frying pan and, when hot, fry the shallots, garlic and chillies for 4–5 minutes or until they are lightly browned.

Toss the salad leaves, coriander leaves and bean sprouts with the tamarind mixture in a large bowl. Divide between 4 plates. Cut the fried eggs in half and arrange on top of the leaves. Sprinkle over the shallot mixture and serve immediately.

For spicy seafood salad, replace the eggs with prawns. Use 20 raw tiger prawns, peeled and deveined but with the tails left intact. Fry the raw prawns in the hot oil for 1–2 minutes until translucent and cooked through. Lightly toss through the tamarind salad mix just before serving.

gram flour rolls

Serves **4**

Preparation time **10 minutes**

Cooking time **20 minutes**

2 tablespoons **sunflower oil**

4 tablespoons **gram flour**
  (besan)

1 tablespoon **natural yogurt**

2 teaspoons sea **salt**

¼ teaspoon ground **turmeric**

¼ teaspoon **asafoetida**

1 teaspoon **chilli powder**

500 ml (17 fl oz) **water**

8–10 **curry leaves**

2 teaspoons **mustard seeds**

1 tablespoon grated fresh
  coconut

1 tablespoon chopped fresh
  coriander leaves

Lightly oil a 30 x 30 cm (12 x 12 inch) baking sheet. In a bowl, whisk together the flour, yogurt, salt, turmeric, asafoetida, chilli powder and measured water. Pour the mixture into a heavy-based saucepan and bring to the boil, stirring occasionally.

Reduce the heat and cook, stirring frequently, for 10–15 minutes or until thick. Remove from the heat and spoon the mixture on to the prepared baking sheet, spreading it thinly over the surface with the back of a wide spoon. Leave for 5–10 minutes to cool, then cut into 2.5 cm (1 inch) strips and roll them up. Divide between 4 plates.

Heat the remaining oil in a small pan and add the curry leaves and mustard seeds. As soon as the seeds start to pop, spoon the oil over the rolls. Sprinkle over the coconut and coriander and serve hot or cold.

For tomato & gram roll salad, toss together 300 g (10 oz) sliced tomatoes, 1 sliced red onion, 1 sliced cucumber and the cooked gram flour rolls.

prawn & mango kebabs

Serves **4**

Preparation time **10 minutes**, plus marinating

Cooking time **4–5 minutes**

16 large raw **tiger prawns**, peeled and deveined

1 tablespoon **sunflower oil**

4 tablespoons **lemon juice**

2 **garlic cloves**, crushed

1 teaspoon grated fresh **root ginger**

1 teaspoon **chilli powder**

1 tablespoon clear **honey**

1 teaspoon **sea salt**

1 large **mango**, peeled, stoned and cut into 16 bite-sized pieces

Put the prawns into a large bowl and add the oil, lemon juice, garlic, ginger, chilli powder, honey and salt. Mix well and marinate for about 10 minutes.

Remove the prawns from the marinade and thread 2 prawns alternately between 2 pieces of mango on each of 8 presoaked wooden skewers.

Place the skewers under a preheated hot grill, brush with the remaining marinade and grill for 2 minutes on each side or until the prawns turn pink and are cooked through. Serve 2 skewers per person with some dressed mixed leaf salad, if liked.

For prawn & pineapple kebabs, replace the mango with ripe pineapple. Peel the pineapple, remove any woody sections of core and cut into large chunks and proceed as above.

tomato salad

Serves **4**

Preparation time **15 minutes**, plus standing

1 **red onion**, finely chopped

4 ripe **tomatoes**, finely chopped

1 **cucumber**, finely chopped

1 **red chilli**, deseeded and finely chopped

small handful of fresh **coriander**, finely chopped

4 tablespoons **lemon juice**

50 g (2 oz) **roasted peanuts**, roughly chopped

salt and **pepper**

Place the onion, tomatoes, cucumber, chilli and coriander into a bowl and pour over the lemon juice. Season well, cover and allow to stand at room temperature for 10–15 minutes.

Before serving, stir to mix well and sprinkle over the chopped nuts. Serve with toasted pappadoms or hot Naan (see page 224).

For tomato raita to accompany any spiced curry or rice dish, omit the peanuts and the lemon juice. Before serving whisk 200 g (7 oz) natural yogurt and stir it into the prepared salad just before serving.

warm cabbage salad

Serves **4**
Preparation time **10 minutes**
Cooking time **5–7 minutes**

2 tablespoons **sunflower oil**
2 teaspoons **black mustard seeds**
1 tablespoon finely grated fresh **root ginger**
10–12 **curry leaves**
1 small **white cabbage**, halved, cored and finely shredded
2–3 tablespoons grated fresh **coconut**
salt and **pepper**
2 tablespoons chopped **roasted peanuts**, to garnish

Heat the oil in a large frying pan or wok and add the mustard seeds. When they start to pop, add the ginger, curry leaves and cabbage and stir-fry over a high heat for 4–5 minutes.

Add the grated coconut and stir-fry for a further 1–2 minutes. Season well and serve immediately.

For sweet fennel & cabbage salad, use ½ small white cabbage, halved, cored and finely shredded, 1 head fennel, finely shredded, and 1 large carrot, peeled and coarsely grated. Add these to the pan with the ginger and curry leaves. Proceed as above.

vegetable samosas

Makes **12**

Preparation time **20 minutes**

Cooking time **15–20 minutes**

3 large **potatoes**, boiled and
roughly mashed

100 g (3½ oz) cooked **peas**

1 teaspoon **cumin seeds**

1 teaspoon **amchoor** (dried
mango powder)

2 fresh **green chillies**,
deseeded and finely
chopped

1 small **red onion**, finely
chopped

3 tablespoons chopped fresh
coriander

1 tablespoon chopped **mint**
leaves

4 tablespoons **lemon juice**

12 **filo pastry** sheets, each
about 30 x 18 cm
(12 x 7 inches)

melted **butter**, for brushing

salt and **pepper**

In a large bowl, mix together the potatoes, peas,
cumin, amchoor, chillies, onion, coriander, mint and
lemon juice. Season with salt and pepper to taste and
set aside.

Fold each sheet of filo pastry in half lengthways. Put
a large spoonful of the potato mixture at one end and
then fold the corner of the pastry over the mixture,
covering it in a triangular shape. Continue folding over
the triangle of pastry along the length of the pastry
strip to make a neat triangular samosa.

Place the samosas on a greased baking sheet, brush
with melted butter and bake in a preheated oven at
200°C (400°F), Gas Mark 6 for 15–20 minutes or
until golden. These crisp savouries can be made in
advance and frozen. They can then be cooked straight
from the freezer.

Serve with Mango, Apple & Mint Chutney (see
page 232), if liked.

For lamb or beef samosas, fry 200 g (7 oz) minced
lamb or beef of your choice in 1 tablespoon of oil
for 5–6 minutes. Stir in 2 tablespoons mild curry
powder, 50 g (2 oz) tomatoes, chopped, and 50 g
(2 oz) fresh or frozen peas. Season well and stir-fry
for a further 5–6 minutes. Cool the mixture before
preparing your samosas, as above.

spiced courgette fritters

Serves **4**

Preparation time **15 minutes**

Cooking time **10 minutes**

100 g (3½ oz) **gram flour**
  (besan)

1 teaspoon **baking powder**

½ teaspoon ground **turmeric**

2 teaspoons ground **coriander**

1 teaspoon ground **cumin**

1 teaspoon **chilli powder**

250 ml (8 fl oz) **soda water**,
  chilled

625 g (1¼ lb) **courgettes**, cut
  into thick batons

salt

sunflower oil, for deep frying

natural yogurt, to dip

Sift the gram flour, baking powder, turmeric, coriander, cumin and chilli powder into a large mixing bowl. Season with salt and gradually add the soda water to make a thick batter, being careful not to overmix.

Pour sunflower oil into a wok until one-third full and heat to 180–190°C (350–375°F), or until a cube of bread browns in 30 seconds. Dip the courgette batons in the spiced batter and then deep-fry in batches for 1–2 minutes or until crisp and golden. Remove with a slotted spoon and drain on kitchen paper. Serve the courgettes immediately with thick natural yogurt, to dip.

For spicy raita, to serve as an accompaniment, whisk 200 g (7 oz) natural yogurt until smooth. Add 6 tablespoons finely chopped mint, 1 small green chilli, deseeded and finely chopped and ½ teaspoon ground cumin. Season with salt, then sprinkle with chilli to serve. Other options include adding chopped cucumber, chopped tomato or finely diced red onion to the yogurt mix.

mulligatawny soup

Serves **4**

Preparation time **15 minutes**

Cooking time **50 minutes**

50 g (2 oz) **butter**

1 large **onion**, thinly sliced

1 small **carrot**, cut into small dice

1 large **celery** stick, finely chopped

25 g (1 oz) **flour**

2 teaspoons **curry powder**

900 ml (1½ pints) **vegetable stock**

1 large **cooking apple**

2 teaspoons **lemon juice**

25 g (1 oz) cooked **basmati rice**

fresh flat leaf **parsley leaves**, roughly chopped, to garnish

Melt the butter in a saucepan and gently fry the onion, carrot and celery until soft. Do not allow to brown. Stir in the flour and curry powder. Cook for 2 minutes and pour in the stock.

Bring to the boil, stirring constantly. Reduce the heat, cover and simmer gently for 30 minutes, stirring occasionally.

Peel, core and dice the apple, then add to the soup with the lemon juice and rice. Season to taste and simmer for a further 10 minutes. Serve hot garnished with a sprinkling of parsley.

For lamb mulligatawny, cut 500 g (1 lb) boneless shoulder or leg of lamb into bite-sized pieces. Lightly brown the meat for 3–5 minutes before adding the onion, carrot and celery. Proceed as above, but increase the cooking time to 45 minutes or longer, until the lamb is tender, before adding the apples.

gujarati carrot salad

Serves **4**

Preparation time **10 minutes**

Cooking time **2–3 minutes**

500 g (1 lb) **carrots**, coarsely grated

4 tablespoons **lemon juice**

1 tablespoon clear **honey**

1 tablespoon **vegetable oil**

½ teaspoon **dried chilli flakes**

2 teaspoons **black mustard seeds**

4 **curry leaves**

salt

Put the carrots into a serving bowl. Mix the lemon juice and honey together and pour over the carrots. Season with salt.

Heat the oil in a small saucepan and add the chilli flakes, mustard seeds and curry leaves. As soon as the mustard seeds start to pop, remove the saucepan from the heat and pour the dressing over the carrots. Stir well to mix.

For beetroot & carrot salad, replace 250 g (8 oz) of the coarsely grated carrots with 250 g (8 oz) peeled and coarsely grated freshly cooked beetroot and proceed as above.

pea & potato tikkis

Serves **4**
Preparation time **30 minutes**
Cooking time **20 minutes**

1 tablespoon **sunflower oil**,
   plus extra for deep-frying
4 teaspoons **cumin seeds**
1 teaspoon **black mustard
   seeds**
1 small **onion**, finely chopped
2 teaspoons finely grated
   fresh **root ginger**
2 **green chillies**, deseeded
   and chopped
625 g (1¼ lb) **potatoes**, diced
   and boiled
200 g (7 oz) fresh **peas**
4 tablespoons **lemon juice**
6 tablespoons chopped fresh
   coriander
100 g (3½ oz) **gram flour**
   (besan)
25 g (1 oz) **self-raising flour**
50 g (2 oz) **rice flour**
large pinch of ground
   turmeric
2 teaspoons crushed
   coriander seeds
350 ml (12 fl oz) **water**
salt and **pepper**

Heat the oil in a wok over a medium heat.

Add the cumin seeds and mustard seeds and stir-fry for 1–2 minutes. Add the onion, ginger and chillies and cook for 3–4 minutes.

Add the cooked potatoes and peas, and stir-fry for 3–4 minutes. Season well and stir in the lemon juice and coriander leaves. Divide the mixture into 25 portions and shape each one into a ball. Chill until ready to use.

Make the batter by mixing together the gram flour, self-raising flour and rice flour in a bowl. Season and add the turmeric and coriander seeds. Gradually whisk in the measured water to make a smooth and thick batter.

Pour sunflower oil into a wok until one-third full and heat to 180–190°C (350–375°F), or until a cube of bread browns in 30 seconds. Dip the potato balls in the batter and deep-fry in batches for 1–2 minutes or until golden. Drain on kitchen paper and serve warm with mint chutney.

For pea & potato tikki sandwich, try these as a filling in a warm crusty roll, drizzled with cool mint chutney. To make the chutney, blend the following ingredients in a blender or food processor until smooth: 100 ml (3½ fl oz) coconut cream, 200 g (7 oz) natural yogurt, 50 g (2 oz) mint leaves, 1 teaspoon caster sugar, 2 tablespoons lime juice and salt and pepper to taste.

marinated lamb skewers

Serves **4**

Preparation time **20 minutes**,
plus marinating

Cooking time **12–15 minutes**

750 g (1 ½ lb) **lamb fillet**, cut
into bite-sized pieces

2 **shallots**, finely chopped

2 teaspoons finely grated
garlic

2 teaspoons grated fresh **root
ginger**

1 tablespoon ground **cumin**

1 tablespoon ground
coriander

1 tablespoon mild **chilli
powder**

1 tablespoon **fennel seeds**

6 tablespoons finely chopped
fresh **coriander**

2 tablespoons finely chopped
mint leaves

250 g (8 oz) **natural yogurt**

½ teaspoon **sugar**

4 tablespoons **lime juice**

lemon segments, for
squeezing

Place the lamb in a large, non-metallic dish. To make
the marinade, place all the remaining ingredients in a
food processor and blend until smooth. Season well.

Pour the mixture over the lamb, cover and chill for
24–48 hours.

When ready to cook, allow the lamb to come to room
temperature. Divide the lamb pieces between 8–12
metal skewers and place on a baking sheet lined with
nonstick baking paper.

Cook in a preheated oven at 200°C (400°F), Gas
Mark 6 for 12–15 minutes or until tender and cooked
through. Serve hot with Naan (see page 224) and
lemon segments, for squeezing.

For mini lamb skewers with minted cucumber dip,
cut the lamb into smaller pieces and thread just 3 or
4 small chunks on each skewer. To make the minted
cucumber dip, mix 1 tablespoon mint jelly with 200 ml
(7 fl oz) Greek yogurt and 6 tablespoons finely diced
cucumber. Season and sprinkle with roasted cumin
seeds, then chill until ready to use.

lobia salad

Serves **4**

Preparation time **15 minutes**

Cooking time **8–10 minutes**

2 **potatoes**, cut into small
cubes

100 g (3½ oz) **green beans**,
cut into 2.5 cm (1 inch)
pieces

400 g (13 oz) canned **black-
eyed beans**, rinsed and
drained

4 **spring onions**, thinly sliced

1 **green chilli**, deseeded and
finely chopped

1 **tomato**, roughly chopped

handful of **mint leaves**

Dressing

2 tablespoons **light olive oil**

1 tablespoon **lemon juice**

½ teaspoon **chilli powder**

1 teaspoon clear **honey**

salt and **pepper**

Cook the potatoes and green beans in a large
saucepan of boiling water for 8–10 minutes. Drain,
allow to cool and place in a large serving bowl.

Add the black-eyed beans, spring onions, chilli, tomato
and mint leaves.

Combine all the dressing ingredients in a small bowl
and mix well. Pour over the salad, toss to mix well and
serve with hot Bhaturas (see page 228).

For mixed bean salad, use a mixture of red kidney
and cannellini beans – a 400 g (13 oz) can of each –
instead of black-eyed beans. Reduce the potato to
1 medium potato to allow for the additional beans
and proceed as above.

curry puffs

Serves **4**
Preparation time **20 minutes**
Cooking time **20 minutes**

1 tablespoon **sunflower oil**,
plus extra for deep-frying
½ small **onion**, finely chopped
3 **garlic cloves**, crushed
1 teaspoon grated fresh **root
ginger**
1 **red chilli**, deseeded and
finely chopped
2 tablespoons **hot curry
powder**
75 g (3 oz) **minced chicken**
100 g (3½ oz) **mashed
potato**
4 tablespoons chopped fresh
coriander
2 sheets of ready-rolled **puff
pastry**
1 **egg**, lightly beaten
salt and **pepper**

Heat the sunflower oil in a wok and add the onion,
garlic, ginger and chilli. Stir-fry over a medium heat for
2–3 minutes and then add the curry powder and
minced chicken. Stir-fry over a high heat for a further
4–5 minutes or until the meat is browned and just
cooked through.

Transfer the mixture to a bowl and add the mashed
potato and coriander and stir to mix well. Season and
set aside.

Use a 7.5 cm (3 inch) cutter to make 8 rounds of puff
pastry. Place a large spoonful of the mince mixture
into the centre of each pastry round. Brush around the
edges of the pastry with the beaten egg, then fold
the pastry over to enclose the filling. Using the tines
of a fork, press and crimp the edges to seal.

Pour sunflower oil into a wok until one-third full and
heat to 180–190°C (350–375°F), or until a cube of
bread browns in 30 seconds. Deep-fry the puffs in
batches for 2–3 minutes or until puffed up and
golden. Drain on kitchen paper and serve immediately
with tomato ketchup, if liked.

For baked curry puffs, use 75 g (3 oz) cooked ham
instead of the chicken and 100 g (3½ oz) mashed
butternut squash instead of the potato. Place the
prepared parcels on to a baking sheet lined with
nonstick baking paper and cook in a preheated oven
at 220°C (425°F), Gas Mark 7 for 15–20 minutes or
until puffed up and golden in colour.

creamy tandoori chicken kebabs

Serves **4**

Preparation time **15 minutes**, plus marinating

Cooking time **6–8 minutes**

750 g (1½ lb) boneless, skinless **chicken thighs**, cut into bite-sized pieces

150 g (5 oz) **natural yogurt**, lightly whisked

100 ml (3½ fl oz) **single cream**

2 teaspoons crushed **garlic**

2 teaspoons grated fresh **root ginger**

2 tablespoons medium **curry powder**

4 tablespoons **garam masala**

1 teaspoon ground **cardamom seeds**

2 tablespoons **tomato purée**

4 tablespoons **lemon juice**

1 tablespoon **tandoori spice powder**

sunflower oil, for brushing

Red onion salad

4 medium **red onions**

salt and **pepper**

juice of 2 **lemons**

Place the chicken in a large, non-metallic dish. To make the marinade, mix together all the remaining ingredients, season well and pour over the chicken. Cover and chill for 24–48 hours.

When ready to cook, allow the chicken to come to room temperature.

Meanwhile slice the onions into thin rings and place in a large mixing bowl. Season with salt and pepper and squeeze over the juice of the lemons. Cover and allow to stand for 30 minutes before tossing and serving with the kebabs.

Divide the chicken pieces between 8–12 metal skewers, place on a lightly oiled grill rack in a single layer and lightly brush with sunflower oil.

Place the kebabs under a medium-hot grill and cook for 3–4 minutes on each side, or until cooked through. Alternatively, cook in a preheated oven at 200°C (400°F), Gas Mark 6 for 8–10 minutes. Serve with the red onion salad and lime halves for squeezing.

For spicy sunday roast, try marinating a whole chicken in this creamy marinade. Cover and chill for 24–48 hours, then bring back to room temperature before roasting it in a preheated oven at 200°C (400°F), Gas Mark 6 for 1¼ hours or until the chicken is cooked through.

poultry

jungle curry with duck

Serves **4**

Preparation time **20 minutes**

Cooking time **30 minutes**

2 tablespoons **sunflower oil**

625 g (1¼ lb) **duck breast**, sliced into thin strips

400 ml (14 fl oz) **chicken stock**

1 tablespoon **Thai fish sauce**

65 g (2½ oz) canned **bamboo shoots**, rinsed and drained

4 **baby aubergines**, quartered

small handful of **Thai basil** leaves

Curry paste

2 tablespoons **green curry paste**

2 tablespoons finely chopped **lemon grass**

3 **lime leaves**, finely shredded

1 teaspoon **shrimp paste**

6 **garlic cloves**, crushed

5 **shallots**, finely chopped

3 tablespoons finely chopped fresh **coriander root**

4 tablespoons **sunflower oil**

Make the curry paste by blending all the ingredients in a small food processor. (You might need to add a little water to make a smooth paste).

Heat the oil in a large, nonstick wok over a high heat and add the curry paste. Stir-fry for 1–2 minutes and then add the duck. Stir-fry for 4–5 minutes until sealed and then pour in the stock and fish sauce and bring to the boil. Remove the duck from the pan with a slotted spoon, set aside and keep warm.

Add the bamboo shoots and aubergines to the pan and cook for 12–15 minutes or until tender.

Return the meat to the pan and cook gently for 3–4 minutes. Stir in half the basil leaves and remove from the heat. Ladle the curry into deep plates or bowls, garnish with the remaining basil leaves and serve immediately with steamed jasmine rice.

For jungle curry with pigeon, you will need 8 pigeon breasts. Slice them thinly and use in the same way as the duck. Use light soy sauce instead of the Thai fish sauce, and for a crunchy texture, replace the canned bamboo shoots with canned water chestnuts. Cook as above until the pigeon is tender.

chicken kofta curry

Serves **4**

Preparation time **25 minutes**,
   plus chilling

Cooking time **45 minutes**

2 teaspoons grated fresh **root
   ginger**

4 teaspoons crushed **garlic**

1 teaspoon ground **cinnamon**

8 tablespoons chopped fresh
   coriander, plus extra to
   garnish

750 g (1 ½ lb) **minced
   chicken**

3 tablespoons **sunflower oil**

1 **onion**, finely chopped

2 tablespoons medium
   curry paste

400 g (13 oz) canned
   chopped tomatoes

200 ml (7 fl oz) **chicken stock**

Place the ginger, garlic, cinnamon, coriander and chicken in a mixing bowl. Season and use your fingers to mix well.

Roll tablespoons of the mixture into bite-sized balls, place on a tray, cover and chill for 1–2 hours.

Heat 2 tablespoons of the oil in a large, nonstick frying pan, add the chicken balls and cook in batches until lightly browned. Remove with a slotted spoon and set aside.

Add the remaining oil to the pan and place over a medium heat. Add the onion and stir-fry for 4–5 minutes and then stir in the curry paste. Stir-fry for 1–2 minutes and then add the tomatoes and stock. Bring to the boil, reduce the heat to low and allow to simmer gently, uncovered, for 10–15 minutes.

Add the chicken balls to the pan and stir gently to coat with the sauce. Simmer gently for 10–15 minutes or until cooked through. Remove from the heat and garnish with chopped coriander before serving.

For creamy chicken kofta curry, stir 150 ml (¼ pint) single cream into the curry sauce 2 minutes before the end of cooking. Heat gently to bring back to the boil before serving. Sprinkle with 2 tablespoons toasted chopped cashew nuts instead of chopped coriander before serving.

tandoori chicken

Serves **4**

Preparation time **10 minutes**, plus marinating

Cooking time **20 minutes**

4 large **chicken quarters**, skinned

200 g (7 oz) **natural yogurt**

1 teaspoon grated fresh **root ginger**

2 **garlic cloves**, crushed

1 teaspoon **garam masala**

2 teaspoons ground **coriander**

¼ teaspoon ground **turmeric**

1 tablespoon **tandoori spice powder**

4 tablespoons **lemon juice**

1 tablespoon **vegetable oil**

salt

lime or **lemon** wedges, to garnish

Place the chicken in a non-metallic, shallow, ovenproof dish and make 3 deep slashes in each piece, to allow the flavours to penetrate. Set aside.

In a bowl, mix together the yogurt, ginger, garlic, garam masala, ground coriander, turmeric, tandoori spice powder, lemon juice and oil. Season with salt and spread the mixture over the chicken pieces to cover. Cover and marinate overnight in the refrigerator, if time allows.

Bake the chicken in a preheated oven at 240°C (475°F), Gas Mark 9 for 20 minutes or until cooked through. Remove from the oven and serve hot, garnished with lime or lemon wedges.

For lettuce, cucumber & onion salad to serve as an accompaniment, combine ½ iceberg lettuce, shredded, ½ mild onion, thinly sliced and separated into pieces and ½ cucumber, lightly peeled, halved lengthways and sliced. Toss with lemon juice and serve on the side with the tandoori chicken.

chicken makhani

Serves **4**

Preparation time **30 minutes**,
  plus marinating

Cooking time 1¼ **hours**

150 g (5 oz) unsalted
  cashews
2 tablespoons medium **curry
  powder**
4 **garlic cloves**, crushed
2 teaspoons finely grated
  fresh **root ginger**
2 tablespoons **white wine
  vinegar**
100 g (3½ oz) **tomato purée**
150 g (5 oz) **natural yogurt**
750 g (1½ lb) boneless,
  skinless **chicken thighs**,
  cut into bite-sized pieces
50 g (2 oz) **butter**
1 **onion**, finely chopped
1 **cinnamon stick**
4 **green cardamom pods**
1 teaspoon **chilli powder**
400 g (13 oz) canned
  chopped tomatoes
150 ml (¼ pint) **chicken stock**
100 ml (3½ fl oz) **single cream**
4 tablespoons chopped fresh
  coriander, to garnish

In a nonstick frying pan, dry-roast the cashews and curry powder over a low heat for 2–3 minutes. Transfer to a coffee grinder and blend until smooth.

Add this mixture to a food processor or blender with the garlic, ginger, vinegar, tomato purée and half the yogurt. Process until smooth. Transfer to a mixing bowl with the remaining yogurt and the chicken. Mix well, cover and marinate in the refrigerator for 24 hours.

Melt the butter in a large nonstick pan and add the onion, cinnamon and cardamom pods. Stir-fry over a medium heat for 6–8 minutes or until the onion is soft. Add the chicken mixture and cook, stirring, for 10 minutes. Season to taste.

Stir in the chilli powder, tomatoes and stock, bring to the boil and reduce the heat. Simmer, uncovered, for 40–45 minutes, stirring occasionally. Add the cream and cook gently for 4–5 minutes. Garnish with the chopped coriander and a drizzle of single cream. Serve immediately with boiled rice or Naan (see page 224).

For lamb & aubergine makhani, replace the chicken with 500 g (1 lb) lean boneless lamb, cubed. Add 1 large aubergine, diced, before mixing in the chilli powder. Finish as above.

burmese chicken noodle curry

Serves **4**
Preparation time **20 minutes**
Cooking time **about 1 hour**

1 kg (2 lb) boneless, skinless
  chicken thighs, cut into
  bite-sized pieces
2 **onions**, chopped
5 **garlic cloves**, chopped
1 teaspoon finely grated fresh
  root ginger
2 tablespoons **sunflower oil**
½ teaspoon **Burmese shrimp
  paste** (belacan)
400 ml (14 fl oz) **coconut
  milk**
1 tablespoon medium **curry
  powder**
200 g (7 oz) **dried rice
  vermicelli**
salt and **pepper**

To garnish

chopped fresh **coriander**
finely chopped **red onion**
fried **garlic** slivers
sliced **red chillies**
lime wedges

Season the chicken pieces and set aside. Process the onion, garlic and ginger in a food processor until smooth. If necessary, add a little water to assist in blending the mixture. Heat the oil in a large pan. Add the onion mixture and shrimp paste and cook, stirring, over a high heat for about 5 minutes.

Add the chicken and cook over a medium heat, turning it until it browns.

Pour in the coconut milk and add the curry powder. Bring to the boil, reduce the heat and simmer, covered, for about 30 minutes, stirring from time to time. Uncover the pan and cook for a further 15 minutes or until the chicken is tender.

Place the noodles in a bowl, cover with boiling water and set aside for 10 minutes. Drain the noodles and divide them between 4 large warmed serving bowls. Ladle over the curry, and garnish with chopped coriander, chopped red onion, fried garlic slivers, sliced red chillies and lime wedges.

For pork & prawn noodle curry, replace the chicken with 450 g (14½ oz) lean boneless pork, then add 100 g (3½ oz) cooked peeled prawns to the curry 5 minutes before the end of cooking. Finish as above.

cashew nut chicken

Serves **4**
Preparation time **10 minutes**
Cooking time **20 minutes**

1 **onion,** roughly chopped
2 tablespoons **tomato purée**
50 g (2 oz) **cashew nuts**
2 teaspoons **garam masala**
2 **garlic cloves**, crushed
1 tablespoon **lemon juice**
¼ teaspoon ground **turmeric**
2 teaspoons **sea salt**
1 tablespoon **natural yogurt**
2 tablespoons **vegetable oil**
3 tablespoons chopped fresh
   coriander leaves, plus extra
   to garnish
50 g (2 oz) **dried apricots**,
   chopped
500 g (1 lb) **chicken thighs**,
   skinned, boned and cut into
   bite-sized pieces
300 ml (½ pint) **chicken stock**

To serve
steamed **rice**
pappadom

Put the onion, tomato purée, cashew nuts, garam masala, garlic, lemon juice, turmeric, salt and yogurt into a food processor or blender and process until fairly smooth. Set aside.

Heat the oil in a large, nonstick frying pan. When hot, pour in the spice mixture. Fry, stirring, for 2 minutes over a medium heat.

Add half the chopped coriander, the apricots and chicken to the pan and stir-fry for 1 minute.

Pour in the chicken stock, cover and simmer for 10–12 minutes or until the chicken is cooked through and tender.

Stir in the remaining chopped coriander and serve with steamed rice and pappadom.

For almond chicken with chickpeas, use almonds instead of cashews and add 400 g (13 oz) canned chickpeas when you add the chicken stock.

spinach & chicken curry

Serves **4**

Preparation time **15 minutes**, plus marinating

Cooking time **1 hour**

5 tablespoons **natural yogurt**
2 tablespoons crushed **garlic**
2 tablespoons grated fresh **root ginger**
1 tablespoon ground **coriander**
1 tablespoon mild **curry powder**
750 g (1½ lb) boneless, skinless **chicken thighs**, cut into bite-sized pieces
400 g (13 oz) frozen whole-leaf **spinach**, thawed
2 tablespoons **sunflower oil**
1 **onion**, finely chopped
2 teaspoons **cumin seeds**
100 ml (3½ fl oz) **water**
1 tablespoon **lemon juice**
salt and **pepper**

Mix together the yogurt, garlic, ginger, ground coriander and curry powder. Season well. Place the chicken in a large, non-metallic bowl and pour over the yogurt mixture. Toss to mix well, cover and marinate in the refrigerator for 8–10 hours.

Place the spinach in a saucepan and cook over a medium heat for 6–8 minutes. Season and drain thoroughly. Place the cooked spinach in a food processor and blend until smooth.

Heat the oil in a large nonstick frying pan and add the onion. Cook over a gentle heat for 10–12 minutes, then add the cumin seeds and stir-fry for 1 minute. Increase the heat to high, add the chicken mixture and stir-fry for 6–8 minutes. Pour in the measured water and the spinach and bring to the boil.

Reduce the heat to low, cover tightly and cook for 25–30 minutes or until the chicken is cooked through.

Uncover the pan, check the seasoning and cook over a high heat for 3–4 minutes, stirring constantly. Remove from the heat and stir in the lemon juice. Serve immediately.

For cauliflower & chicken curry, substitute

½ a cauliflower for the spinach. Cut the cauliflower into small florets, and halve the larger florets. Proceed as above, adding the cauliflower to the curry when you add the water.

thai barbecued chicken

Serves **4**

Preparation time **15 minutes**,
plus marinating

Cooking time **10–25 minutes**

1.5 kg (3 lb) part-boned
chicken breasts

5 cm (2 in) piece of fresh
galangal, peeled and finely
chopped

4 **garlic cloves**, crushed

1 large **red chilli**, finely
chopped

4 **shallots**, finely chopped

2 tablespoons finely chopped
coriander leaves

150 ml (½ pint) **thick coconut
milk**

salt and **pepper**

To garnish
lime wedges
chive flowers (optional)

Rub the chicken breasts all over with salt and pepper
and place in a shallow dish.

Put the galangal, garlic, red chilli, shallots and fresh
coriander in a food processor and blend to a paste or
use a pestle and mortar. Add the coconut milk and mix
until well combined.

Pour this marinade over the chicken, cover and leave
to marinate overnight in the refrigerator.

Remove the chicken from the marinade and place on
a hot barbecue or griddle pan. Cook for 10–25 minutes,
turning and basting regularly with the remaining
coconut marinade.

Leave the chicken to rest for 5 minutes then chop
into small pieces with a cleaver. Garnish with lime
wedges and chive flowers, if liked. Serve with a
ready-made sweet chilli sauce and Fragrant Coconut
Rice (see page 206).

For Thai barbecue spatchcocked chicken, replace
the chicken with the same weight of butterflied
spatchcocked chicken. Increase the cooking time
to 30–40 minutes. The chicken is properly cooked
when a skewer is inserted in one of the legs and
clear juices run out.

mustard chicken

Serves **4**
Preparation time **15 minutes**
Cooking time **35–40 minutes**

2 tablespoons **sunflower oil**
1 **onion**, thinly sliced
2 teaspoons **brown mustard seeds**
2 teaspoons crushed **garlic**
1 teaspoon ground **turmeric**
2 teaspoons ground **coriander**
2 tablespoons **mild curry powder**
750 g (1½ lb) boneless, skinless **chicken thighs**
250 ml (8 fl oz) **water**
6 tablespoons **natural yogurt**, lightly whisked
salt and **pepper**
fresh **coriander leaves**, to garnish

Heat the oil in a large, nonstick wok or frying pan. Add the onion and stir-fry over a medium heat for 5–6 minutes until softened.

Pound the mustard seeds with the garlic using a pestle and mortar and add to the pan. Stir-fry for 1 minute, then add the turmeric, ground coriander and curry powder. Stir-fry for 2–3 minutes, then add the chicken. Stir-fry over a high heat for 5 minutes, then add the measured water. Season well.

Bring to the boil, cover tightly and reduce the heat to low. Cook gently for 20–25 minutes, stirring occasionally until the chicken is cooked through. Remove from the heat and stir in the yogurt.

Serve immediately with pilau rice and garnished with coriander leaves.

For fiery chicken curry, add 4 dried red chillies, 1 cinnamon stick, 2 cloves and 1 star anise to the mustard seeds and garlic when you grind the spice mixture. Serve with a bowl of yogurt flavoured with chopped fresh mint as an accompaniment. To make this whisk 250 g (8 oz) natural yogurt with 4 tablespoons finely chopped fresh mint.

aromatic chicken pilaf

Serves **4**
Preparation time **15 minutes**,
  plus standing
Cooking time **25 minutes**

1 tablespoon **sunflower oil**
1 **onion**, sliced
1 **garlic clove**, chopped
1 **red pepper**, deseeded and
  chopped
1 teaspoon **cumin seeds**
1 teaspoon ground **coriander**
2 teaspoons **chilli powder**
2 teaspoons **curry powder**
4 large **chicken thighs**,
  cut into bite-sized pieces
200 g (7 oz) **basmati rice**
600 ml (1 pint) **chicken stock**
125 g (4 oz) ready-to-eat
  dried apricots, chopped
3 tablespoons chopped fresh
  coriander
4 tablespoons **natural yogurt**

Heat the oil in a nonstick frying pan, add the onion,
garlic and red pepper and stir-fry for 3–4 minutes
until softened.

Add the spices and continue to fry for 1 minute, then
add the chicken and cook for 2 minutes until browned
all over. Add the rice to the pan and stir to combine.

Stir in the chicken stock and apricots, cover tightly
and simmer for 15 minutes until the rice is cooked
through and the chicken is tender. Leave to stand,
covered, for 5 minutes.

Scatter over the coriander and top each serving with
a spoonful of yogurt. Serve immediately.

For special chicken pilaf, fold in 50 g (2 oz) slivered
almonds and 3 hard-boiled eggs, cut into eighths,
when the pilaf is cooked. The dried apricots can also
be replaced with the same weight of sultanas.

lemon grass chicken

Serves **4**

Preparation time **15 minutes**

Cooking time **1¾–2¼ hours**

1 tablespoon **sunflower oil**

12 large **chicken drumsticks**

1 **onion**, finely chopped

4 **garlic cloves**, crushed

6 tablespoons very finely chopped **lemon grass**

1 **lemon grass stalk**, halved lengthways

1 **red chilli**, finely sliced or chopped

2 tablespoons **medium curry paste**

1 tablespoon grated **palm sugar**

250 ml (8 fl oz) **chicken stock**

salt and **pepper**

Heat the oil in a large, heavy-based casserole dish and brown the drumsticks evenly for 5–6 minutes. Remove with a slotted spoon and set aside.

Add the onion and stir-fry over a low heat for 10 minutes. Add the garlic, lemon grass, chilli and curry paste and stir-fry for 1–2 minutes.

Return the chicken to the dish with the palm sugar and stock. Bring to the boil, season and cover tightly. Cook in a preheated oven at 140°C (275°F), Gas Mark 1 for 1½–2 hours or until tender. Remove from the oven and serve immediately.

For lemon grass beef, use 750 g (1½ lb) stewing beef, cut into large cubes, in place of the chicken. Increase the cooking time to 2½–3 hours for thoroughly tender beef. Serve with a fresh mango salad of 1 large diced mango dressed with the rind and juice of 1 lime.

swahili chicken

Serves **4**

Preparation time **20 minutes**, plus marinating

Cooking time **1½ hours**

1 **chicken**, cut into 8 pieces

4 teaspoons finely grated fresh **root ginger**

6 **garlic cloves**, crushed

2 teaspoons ground **turmeric**

1 tablespoon **paprika**

1 teaspoon ground **cinnamon**

8 tablespoons **lemon juice**

4 tablespoons **sunflower oil**

2 teaspoons ground **cumin**

1 tablespoon ground **coriander**

2 teaspoons **dried chilli flakes**

100 g (3½ oz) **natural yogurt**, whisked

1 tablespoon runny **honey**

salt and **pepper**

Place the chicken pieces in a large mixing bowl. Mix together the remaining ingredients, season well and pour over the chicken. Mix well to combine, cover and marinate in the refrigerator for 6–8 hours or overnight if time permits.

Place the chicken mixture in a shallow, lightly oiled, ovenproof baking dish and cook in a preheated oven at 150°C (300°F), Gas Mark 2 for 1½ hours, covering the dish with foil for the last 30–40 minutes of cooking. Serve accompanied by plain boiled rice or flat bread, if liked.

For Swahili chicken drumsticks with cumin dip,

use 12 chicken drumsticks instead of the whole chicken and proceed as above. To make it easier to eat the drumsticks with your fingers, only cover the chicken with foil when the dish is quite dry. Serve at room temperature with minted yogurt for dipping. To make this whisk 250 g (8 oz) natural yogurt with ¼ teaspoon ground cumin and 4 tablespoons finely chopped fresh mint. Season well then chill until ready to serve.

chicken & baby spinach curry

Serves **4**

Preparation time **10 minutes**

Cooking time **25 minutes**

1 tablespoon **sunflower oil**

4 boneless, skinless **chicken breasts**, halved lengthways

1 **onion**, sliced

2 **garlic cloves**, chopped

1 **green chilli**, chopped

4 **cardamom pods**, lightly crushed

1 teaspoon **cumin seeds**

1 teaspoon **dried chilli flakes**

1 teaspoon ground **ginger**

1 teaspoon ground **turmeric**

250 g (8 oz) **baby leaf spinach**

300 g (10 oz) **tomatoes**, chopped

150 g (5 oz) **natural yogurt**

2 tablespoons chopped fresh **coriander**

Heat the oil in a large nonstick saucepan or frying pan. Add the chicken, onion, garlic and chilli and fry for 4–5 minutes until the chicken begins to brown and the onion to soften.

Add the cardamom pods, cumin seeds, chilli flakes, ginger and turmeric and continue to fry for 1 minute.

Add the spinach to the pan, cover and cook gently until the spinach wilts, then stir in the tomatoes and simmer for 15 minutes, removing the lid for the last 5 minutes.

Stir in the yogurt and chopped coriander and serve with basmati rice.

For chicken & pea curry, use 200 g (7 oz) fresh or frozen peas, adding them to the curry with the tomatoes. Sprinkle with 1 tablespoon chopped fresh mint as well as the coriander before serving.

green chicken curry

Serves **4**

Preparation time **15 minutes**

Cooking time **30–35 minutes**

1 tablespoon **sunflower oil**

3 tablespoons **Thai green curry paste**

2 **green chillies**, finely chopped

750 g (1½ lb) boneless, skinless **chicken thighs**, cut into bite-sized pieces

400 ml (14 fl oz) **coconut milk**

200 ml (7 fl oz) **chicken stock**

6 **lime leaves**

2 tablespoons **Thai fish sauce**

1 tablespoon grated **palm sugar**

200 g (7 oz) **pea aubergines**, or standard aubergine, diced

100 g (3½ oz) **green beans**, trimmed

50 g (2 oz) canned **bamboo shoots**, rinsed and drained

large handful **Thai basil leaves**

large handful of fresh **coriander leaves**

4 tablespoons **lime juice**

Heat the oil in a large nonstick wok or saucepan and add the curry paste and chillies. Stir-fry for 2–3 minutes and then add the chicken. Stir and cook for 5–6 minutes or until the chicken is sealed and lightly browned.

Stir in the coconut milk, stock, lime leaves, fish sauce, palm sugar and pea aubergines. Simmer, uncovered for 10–15 minutes, stirring occasionally.

Add the green beans and bamboo shoots and continue to simmer for 6–8 minutes.

Remove from the heat and stir in the herbs and lime juice. Serve ladled into warmed bowls accompanied by steamed jasmine rice, if liked.

For homemade Thai green curry paste, blend the following ingredients to a smooth paste in a food processor: 4–6 long green chillies, chopped, 2 tablespoons chopped garlic, 2 tablespoons chopped lemon grass stalks, 4 shallots, finely chopped, 1 tablespoon finely chopped galangal or fresh root ginger, 2 teaspoons finely chopped lime leaves, 2 teaspoons ground coriander, 2 teaspoons ground cumin, 1 teaspoon white peppercorns, 2 teaspoons shrimp paste and 1 tablespoon groundnut oil. Store in an airtight container in the refrigerator for up to one month.

pork and beef

calcutta beef curry

Serves **4**

Preparation time **20 minutes**,
  plus marinating

Cooking time **1 hour
  20 minutes**

400 g (13 oz) **stewing beef**,
  cut into bite-sized pieces
5 tablespoons **natural yogurt**
1 tablespoon medium **curry
  powder**
2 tablespoons **mustard oil**
1 dried **bay leaf**
1 **cinnamon stick**
3 **cloves**
4 green **cardamom pods**,
  bruised
1 large **onion**, halved and
  thinly sliced
3 **garlic cloves**, crushed
1 teaspoon finely grated fresh
  root ginger
1 teaspoon ground **turmeric**
1 teaspoon hot **chilli powder**
2 teaspoons ground **cumin**
400 ml (14 fl oz) **beef stock**
salt

Place the meat in a non-metallic bowl. Mix together the yogurt and curry powder and pour over the meat. Season with salt, cover and marinate in the refrigerator for 24 hours.

Heat the oil in a large nonstick wok or frying pan and add the spices. Stir-fry for 1 minute and then add the onion. Stir-fry over a medium heat for 4–5 minutes, then add the garlic, ginger, turmeric, chilli powder and cumin. Add the marinated meat and stir-fry for 10–15 minutes over a low heat.

Pour in the beef stock and bring to the boil. Reduce the heat to low, cover tightly and simmer gently, stirring occasionally, for 1 hour or until the meat is tender. Check the seasoning, remove from the heat and serve immediately with rice and pickles, if liked.

For Calcutta chicken curry, use 4 chicken thighs and 4 chicken drumsticks instead of the beef. Also replace the beef stock with chicken stock. Follow the same instructions as the recipe above. Add 100 g (3½ oz) sliced ready-to-eat dried apricots for a hint of sweetness, stirring them in with the stock.

red beef curry

Serves **4**

Preparation time **20 minutes**

Cooking time **1¾ hours**

400 g (13 oz) **fillet steak**

1 tablespoon **sunflower oil**

2 tablespoons **Thai red curry paste**

400 ml (14 fl oz) **coconut milk**

200 ml (7 fl oz) **beef stock**

2 tablespoons **Thai fish sauce**

1 tablespoon **lime juice**

6 **lime leaves**, finely shredded

2 **courgettes**, thinly sliced

200 g (7 oz) canned **bamboo shoots**, rinsed and drained

small handful of **Thai basil leaves**

salt

Place the steak on a work surface and cover with clingfilm. Use a mallet to beat the steak until it is about 1 cm (½ inch) thick. Cut the beef into thin strips and set aside.

Heat the oil in a large, heavy-based saucepan. Add the beef strips in batches and stir-fry for 2–3 minutes until browned. Remove with a slotted spoon and set aside.

Add the curry paste to the saucepan and stir-fry for 2–3 minutes over a medium heat. Add the coconut milk, stock, fish sauce, lime juice, lime leaves and the beef. Bring to the boil, turn the heat to low and simmer, uncovered, for 1 hour.

Add the courgettes and bamboo shoots and continue to cook gently for 20–25 minutes. Season and remove from the heat. Stir in the basil leaves just before serving with steamed rice.

For homemade Thai red curry paste, process the following ingredients to a smooth paste in a food processor: 8 long red chillies, deseeded and finely chopped, 1 teaspoon white peppercorns, 3 fresh coriander roots, finely chopped, 1 teaspoon ground cumin, 2 teaspoons ground coriander, 2 tablespoons finely chopped garlic, 2 tablespoons finely chopped lemon grass stalks, 2 teaspoons finely chopped lime leaves, 1 tablespoon finely chopped galangal or fresh root ginger, 2 teaspoons shrimp paste and 2 tablespoons sunflower oil. Store in an airtight container in the refrigerator for up to one month.

nonya meatball curry

Serves **4**

Preparation time **25 minutes**, plus chilling

Cooking time **30 minutes**

3 teaspoons crushed **garlic**

100 g (3½ oz) **shallots**, finely chopped

1 teaspoon grated **galangal** or fresh **root ginger**

6 long **red chillies**, plus extra for garnish

6 tablespoons **sunflower oil**

400 g (13 oz) canned **chopped tomatoes**

1 tablespoon **kecap asin**

400 ml (14 fl oz) **coconut milk**

salt and **pepper**

chopped fresh **coriander**, to garnish

Meatballs

2 **eggs**

2 teaspoons **cornflour**

2 **garlic cloves**, crushed

2 tablespoons finely chopped fresh **coriander**

2 **red chillies**, finely chopped

750 g (1½ lb) **minced beef**

Make the meatballs by combining all the ingredients together in a large mixing bowl. Season well and roll tablespoons of the mixture into walnut-sized balls. Place on a tray, cover and chill for 3–4 hours or overnight if time permits.

Place the garlic, shallots, galangal or ginger, chillies and half the oil in a small food processor and blend to a paste.

Heat the remaining oil in a large nonstick wok, add the paste and stir-fry for 1–2 minutes. Add the tomatoes, kecap asin and coconut milk and bring to the boil. Reduce the heat to low and simmer gently for 10 minutes.

Add the meatballs to the curry and simmer for 12–15 minutes, stirring occasionally. Remove from the heat and serve with rice noodles or steamed rice, as preferred. Garnish with sliced red chillies and chopped coriander.

For pork meatball curry, replace the minced beef with the same quantity of minced pork, and instead of kecap asin substitute 1 tablespoon dark soy sauce and 1 teaspoon Thai fish sauce. Cook as above.

kheema mutter

Serves **4**
Preparation time **20 minutes**
Cooking time **1½–2 hours**

2 tablespoons **sunflower oil**
1 large **onion**, finely chopped
3 **garlic cloves**, crushed
1 teaspoon finely grated fresh
   root ginger
3–4 **green chillies**, deseeded
   and finely sliced
1 tablespoon **cumin seeds**
3 tablespoons hot **curry paste**
750 g (1½ lb) **minced beef**
400 g (13 oz) canned
   chopped tomatoes
1 teaspoon **sugar**
4 tablespoons **tomato purée**
4 tablespoons **coconut cream**
250 g (8 oz) fresh or frozen
   peas
salt and **pepper**
large handful of chopped fresh
   coriander, to garnish

Heat the oil in a large, heavy-based saucepan and add the onion. Cook over a low heat for 15–20 minutes, until softened and just turning light golden-brown. Add the garlic, ginger, chilli, cumin seeds and curry paste and stir-fry over a high heat for 1–2 minutes.

Add the minced beef and stir-fry for 3–4 minutes. Stir in the tomatoes, sugar and tomato purée and bring to the boil. Season well, cover and reduce the heat to low. Cook for 1–1½ hours until the mince is tender.

Pour in the coconut cream and add the peas 10 minutes before the end of cooking time. Garnish with the chopped coriander and serve lime slices and red chillies as well as rice or Naan (see page 224), if liked.

For spaghetti with spicy mince & peas, use this dish as a tasty pasta sauce. Cook 325 g (11 oz) spaghetti in boiling salted water for 12–15 minutes, then drain and divide among four plates. Ladle the sauce over and serve.

cambodian pork curry

Serves **4**
Preparation time **20 minutes**
Cooking time **1 hour**

2 tablespoons **sunflower oil**
6 **shallots**, finely chopped
1 **red chilli**, thinly sliced
2 teaspoons grated **galangal**
   or fresh **root ginger**
2 teaspoons crushed **garlic**
2 teaspoons crushed
   fenugreek seeds
1 tablespoon ground **cumin**
1 teaspoon ground **turmeric**
1 tablespoon **tamarind paste**
finely grated rind and juice of
   1 **lime**
400 ml (14 fl oz) **coconut
   milk**
8 baby **new potatoes**, halved
   if large
2 **red peppers**, cut into bite-
   sized pieces
625 g (1¼ lb) **pork fillet**,
   cut into bite-sized pieces
salt and **pepper**

Heat the oil in a large nonstick wok or frying pan. Add the shallots, chilli, galangal or ginger, garlic, fenugreek, cumin and turmeric and stir-fry for 3–4 minutes.

Stir in the tamarind, lime rind and juice, coconut milk, potatoes and red pepper and bring to the boil.

Reduce the heat and simmer, covered, for 25 minutes, stirring occasionally.

Add the pork, season well and simmer gently, uncovered, for 25 minutes or until the pork is tender.

Serve hot ladled into warmed bowls with rice.

For cambodian pork & courgette curry, use 2 large sliced courgettes in place of the red peppers. Slice the courgettes and add to the curry 10 minutes after you add the pork.

For tamarind paste, place the dried tamarind pods in a heatproof jug and cover with boiling water. Allow to infuse for 30 minutes, then sieve the mixture to get a paste.

seekh kebabs

Makes **12**
Preparation time **20 minutes**,
  plus chilling
Cooking time **10 minutes**

2 fresh **green chillies**,
  deseeded and finely
  chopped
1 teaspoon grated fresh **root
  ginger**
2 **garlic cloves**, crushed
3 tablespoons chopped fresh
  coriander leaves
2 tablespoons chopped **mint**
  leaves
1 teaspoon **cumin seeds**
1 tablespoon **vegetable oil**,
  plus extra for oiling
½ teaspoon ground **cloves**
½ teaspoon ground
  cardamom seeds
450 g (14½ oz) **minced beef**
salt

Put the chillies, ginger, garlic, coriander, mint, cumin, oil, cloves and cardamom into a food processor or blender and process until fairly smooth.

Transfer to a mixing bowl, add the beef and season with salt. Mix well, preferably with your hands to ensure the beef is evenly seasoned.

Divide the mixture into 12 portions, cover and chill for 30 minutes, if time allows.

Lightly oil 12 flat metal skewers and shape the kebab mixture around each skewer, forming a sausage shape.

Place the kebabs under a preheated hot grill and cook for 3–4 minutes on each side or until cooked through and browned. Serve with sliced red onions, chopped mint and hot bread, if liked

For marinated steak kebabs, use cubes of beef instead of minced beef. Cut 500 g (1 lb) fillet steak into cubes, mix with the spice paste and leave to marinate for several hours. Thread the cubes on the skewers and cook as above. Chunks of green pepper and pieces of quartered onion can be added to the kebabs when skewering the meat.

goan pork vindaloo

Serves **4**

Preparation time **25 minutes**,
  plus marinating

Cooking time **1 hour
  40 minutes**

2 teaspoons roasted **cumin
  seeds**

6 dried **red chillies**

1 teaspoon crushed
  cardamom seeds

1 **cinnamon stick**

10 **black peppercorns**

8 **garlic cloves**, crushed

5 tablespoons **wine vinegar**

625 g (1¼ lb) boneless **pork**,
  cut into bite-sized pieces

2 tablespoons **sunflower oil**

1 **onion**, finely chopped

2 tablespoon hot **curry
  powder**

4 **potatoes**, peeled and
  quartered

6 tablespoons **tomato purée**

1 tablespoon **sugar**

400 g (13 oz) canned
  chopped tomatoes

200 ml (7 fl oz) **chicken stock**

salt and **pepper**

fresh **coriander**, to garnish

Make the spice paste by placing the cumin seeds, dried chillies, cardamom seeds, cinnamon stick, peppercorns, garlic and vinegar into a small food processor and processing into a smooth paste. Place the pork in a non-metallic dish and pour over the paste. Rub into the pork, cover and marinate in the refrigerator for up to 24 hours.

Heat the oil in a large, heavy-based saucepan and add the onion. Stir-fry for 3–4 minutes, then add the curry powder and the pork. Stir-fry for 3–4 minutes and then stir in the potatoes, tomato purée, sugar, chopped tomatoes and stock.

Season well and bring to the boil. Cover tightly and reduce the heat to low. Gently simmer for 1½ hours or until the pork is tender.

Garnish with chopped fresh coriander and serve immediately with steamed white rice.

For papaya & mint raita, to serve as an accompaniment, mix 200 ml (7 fl oz) natural yogurt with a handful of chopped mint leaves. Halve, deseed and peel 1 small papaya, then dice the flesh and mix into the minted yogurt.

massaman beef curry

Serves **4**

Preparation time **20 minutes**

Cooking time **about 2½ hours**

750 g (1½ lb) **stewing beef**, cut into bite-sized pieces

500 ml (17 fl oz) **beef stock**

1 teaspoon **cardamom seeds**

3 **cloves**

3 **star anise**

1 tablespoon grated **palm sugar**

2 tablespoons **Thai fish sauce**

2 tablespoons **tamarind paste**

600 ml (1 pint) **coconut milk**

2 tablespoons **Thai red curry paste**

2 **lemon grass** stalks, bruised

16 **shallots**, peeled

325 g (11 oz) **butternut squash**, peeled and cut into bite-sized pieces

salt and **pepper**

finely chopped **spring onions**, to garnish

Place the beef in a large, heavy-based saucepan with the stock, cardamom, cloves, star anise, palm sugar, fish sauce, half the tamarind paste and half the coconut milk. Bring to the boil, reduce the heat and simmer gently for 2 hours, stirring occasionally.

Strain the beef over a large bowl, reserving the liquid. Cover and keep warm. Meanwhile, return the saucepan to a medium heat and add the curry paste and remaining coconut milk. Bring to the boil and add the remaining tamarind.

Stir in the beef with the lemon grass, shallots, butternut squash and 250 ml (8 fl oz) of the reserved liquid. Simmer, uncovered, for 20–25 minutes. Remove from the heat, season to taste and sprinkle over the spring onions just before serving.

For lamb & potato curry, use the same quantity of diced lamb instead of the beef, and use potatoes instead of the butternut squash. You will need about 400 g (13 oz) potatoes, peeled and cut into 2.5 cm (1 inch) dice. Cook as above.

pork & lemon grass curry

Serves **4**
Preparation time **20 minutes**
Cooking time **40 minutes**

4 tablespoons **sunflower oil**
750 g (1½ lb) **minced pork**
8 tablespoons finely chopped
    lemon grass
3 **garlic cloves**, crushed
2 teaspoons grated **galangal**
    or fresh **root ginger**
1 tablespoon **Thai green
    curry paste**
1 teaspoon ground **turmeric**
2 **green chillies**, chopped
150 ml (¼ pint) **water**
400 ml (14 fl oz) **coconut
    milk**
4 **lime leaves**, finely shredded
200 g (7 oz) **sugarsnap peas**,
    trimmed
2 tablespoons **lime juice**
salt and **pepper**

Heat half the oil in a large, nonstick wok and brown the pork over a high heat for 3–4 minutes. Remove from the wok and set aside.

Place the lemon grass, garlic, galangal or ginger, curry paste, turmeric and chillies in a food processor with the measured water and process until smooth.

Add the remaining oil to the wok and place over a high heat. Add the lemon grass paste and stir-fry for 2–3 minutes, then add the pork and stir-fry for a further 2–3 minutes.

Stir in the coconut milk and lime leaves, season and bring to the boil. Reduce the heat and simmer, uncovered, for 30 minutes, stirring occasionally.

Add the sugarsnap peas 6 minutes before the end of cooking and stir to mix well.

Remove from the heat and stir in the lime juice before serving with rice or noodles.

For pork & vegetable lemon grass curry, use 150 g (5 oz) each of fine green beans and carrots. Cut the carrots into short thin batons. Cook as above, omitting the sugarsnap peas.

spicy pork patties

Makes **12**
Preparation time **20 minutes**,
  plus chilling
Cooking time **20 minutes**

450 g (14½ oz) **minced pork**
3 teaspoons hot **curry paste**
3 tablespoons fresh
  breadcrumbs
1 small **onion**, finely chopped
2 tablespoons **lime juice**
2 tablespoons chopped fresh
  coriander leaves
1 **red chilli**, finely chopped
2 teaspoons grated **palm
  sugar**
sunflower oil, for frying
salt and **pepper**

Put the pork, curry paste, breadcrumbs, onion, lime juice, coriander, chilli and sugar into a large bowl and, using your hands, mix until thoroughly blended. Season with salt and pepper, cover and chill for 30 minutes or until ready to cook.

Divide the mixture into 12 portions and shape each one into a flat, round patty.

Heat the oil in a large, nonstick frying pan and cook the patties over a medium heat for 3–4 minutes on each side or until cooked through. Remove with a slotted spoon and drain on kitchen paper. Serve hot with natural yogurt and chutneys, if liked.

For spicy pork & prawn patties, use 400 g (13 oz) of raw tiger prawns, plus 150 g (5 oz) of minced pork instead of 450 g (14½ oz) pork. Peel and devein the prawns, then chop them finely or process them briefly in a food processor before mixing with the other ingredients. Proceed as above and serve with grated courgette and carrot salad. To make this, coarsely grate 1 large carrot and 1 courgette, then toss with the rind of 1 lime and a squeeze of lime juice.

fragrant vietnamese beef curry

Serves **4**
Preparation time **15 minutes**
Cooking time **15–20 minutes**

3 tablespoons **sunflower oil**
750 g (1 ½ lb) thin-cut **fillet
steak**, cut into strips
1 **onion**, finely sliced
4 **garlic cloves**, finely
chopped
1 **red chilli**, finely sliced
2 **star anise**
1 teaspoon crushed
cardamom seeds
1 **cinnamon stick**
300 g (10 oz) **green beans**,
trimmed
1 **carrot**, cut into thin batons
2 tablespoons **Thai fish
sauce**
2 tablespoons **ground bean
sauce**

To garnish
small handful of finely chopped
fresh **coriander**
small handful of finely chopped
mint leaves

Heat half the oil in a large, nonstick frying pan and
stir-fry the beef in batches for 1–2 minutes. Remove
with a slotted spoon and keep warm.

Heat the remaining oil in the frying pan and stir-fry
the onion for 4–5 minutes until softened, then add the
garlic, chilli, star anise, cardamom, cinnamon, green
beans and carrot. Stir-fry for 6–8 minutes.

Return the beef to the pan with the fish sauce and
the ground bean sauce. Stir-fry for 3–4 minutes or
until heated through. Remove from the heat and
sprinkle over the chopped herbs just before serving.

For stuffed rice paper rolls, soak 8 Bahn Trang
or large rice paper wrappers in warm water for
3–4 minutes or until soft and pliable to handle. Pat
dry with kitchen paper and spread out on a clean
work surface. Thinly shred 6 iceberg lettuce leaves
and divide the lettuce between the prepared rice
paper wrappers. Top each with 3 tablespoons of the
cooked beef curry mixture along the centre of the
wrapper, making sure the pile of filling is compact.
Turn up the bottom of the wrapper to cover the filling
then, holding the filling in place with your fingers,
carefully turn the two sides in and very gently roll up.
Transfer the roll to a serving plate and cover with a
damp cloth or clingfilm while you make the remaining
rolls. Serve as soon as they are made or the
wrappers will dry out and become tough.

aromatic pork belly curry

Serves **4**

Preparation time **20 minutes**

Cooking time **2¾ hours**

3 tablespoons **sunflower oil**

750 g (1½ lb) **pork belly**, cut into bite-sized pieces

10 **curry leaves**

1 tablespoon **cumin seeds**

1 tablespoon **coriander seeds**, crushed

1 **onion**, finely chopped

2 teaspoons finely grated **garlic**

2 teaspoons finely grated fresh **root ginger**

2 tablespoons **medium curry powder**

2 tablespoons **wine vinegar**

2 **cinnamon sticks**

2 **star anise**

6 green **cardamom pods**, bruised

400 ml (14 fl oz) **coconut milk**

200 ml (7 fl oz) **water**

salt and **pepper**

Heat half the oil in a heavy-based frying pan and add the pork. Stir-fry for 4–5 minutes until browned, remove with a slotted spoon and set aside.

Add the remaining oil to the pan and add the curry leaves, cumin, coriander, onion, garlic and ginger. Stir-fry for 3–4 minutes, then return the pork to the pan with the curry powder. Stir-fry for 2–3 minutes more.

Stir in the vinegar, cinnamon, star anise, cardamom and coconut milk and measured water. Season and bring to the boil.

Cover tightly and cook in a preheated oven at 150°C (300°F), Gas Mark 2 for 2½ hours or until the pork is tender. Serve with crusty bread or rice.

For pork curry with pineapple, use the same weight of lean pork loin or shoulder, cut into cubes, and proceed as above. Add a drained 250 g (8 oz) can pineapple chunks to the cooked curry just before serving for a succulent flavour contrast.

bangkok sour pork curry

Serves **4**
Preparation time **20 minutes**
Cooking time **2¼ hours**

1 tablespoon **sunflower oil**
1 **onion**, finely chopped
1 teaspoon finely grated
   galangal or fresh **root**
   ginger
3 tablespoons **Thai red curry**
   paste
750 g (1½ lb) thick **pork**
   steaks, cut into bite-sized
   pieces
750 ml (1¼ pints) **chicken**
   stock
8 tablespoons finely chopped
   fresh **coriander root** and
   stem
2 **lemon grass** stalks, bruised
4 tablespoons **tamarind**
   paste
1 tablespoon grated **palm**
   sugar
6 **lime leaves**

To garnish
small handful **Thai basil** leaves
fresh **lime leaves** (optional)

Heat the oil in a large, heavy-based casserole dish
and fry the onion over a medium heat for 3–4 minutes.
Add the galangal or ginger, curry paste and pork and
stir-fry for 4–5 minutes.

Pour in the stock and add the chopped coriander,
lemon grass, tamarind, palm sugar and lime leaves.
Bring to the boil, remove from the heat, cover and
cook in a preheated oven at 150°C (300°F), Gas
Mark 2 for 2 hours or until the pork is tender.

Scatter over the basil leaves just before serving and
garnish with lime leaves, if liked. Serve with steamed
jasmine rice or Fragrant Coconut Rice (see page 206).

For Bangkok sour pork curry with noodles, use
fresh noodles, available in the chilled section of
Oriental stores and large supermarkets. These have
the best texture, but dried noodles are a good
substitute. Cook 250 g (8 oz) thick egg noodles
according to the instructions on the packet. Divide
them among four bowls and ladle the curry over the
top. Sprinkle with extra chopped fresh coriander as
well as the basil and lime leaves.

lamb

creamy lamb korma

Serves **4**
Preparation time **20 minutes**
Cooking time **45 minutes**

4 tablespoons **sunflower oil**
750 g (1½ lb) **lamb neck fillet**, thinly sliced
1 **onion**, finely chopped
2 **garlic cloves**, finely chopped
2 teaspoons finely grated fresh **root ginger**
65 g (2½ oz) **ground almonds**
1 tablespoon **white poppy seeds** (khus)
5 tablespoons **korma curry paste**
150 ml (¼ pint) **vegetable stock**
250 ml (8 fl oz) **single cream**
salt and **pepper**

To garnish
slivered green **pistachio nuts**
crispy fried **shallots**

Heat half the oil in a large, nonstick frying pan and brown the lamb in batches for 2–3 minutes. Remove with a slotted spoon and set aside.

Add the remaining oil to the pan and add the onion, garlic and ginger and cook over a medium heat for 3–4 minutes. Stir in the ground almonds, poppy seeds and curry paste and stir-fry for 1–2 minutes.

Add the reserved lamb to the pan with the stock and cream. Bring to the boil and season well. Reduce the heat and simmer, uncovered, stirring occasionally, for 30 minutes or until the lamb is tender.

Remove from the heat and garnish with slivered pistachio nuts and crispy fried shallots. Serve immediately with warm Naan (see page 224) or rice.

For vegetable korma, sauté 750 g (1½ lb) of a mixture of cauliflower and broccoli florets for 2–3 minutes in a tablespoon of oil with 4 finely chopped shallots, 2 finely chopped garlic cloves and 1 teaspoon finely grated ginger. Stir in 65 g (2½ oz) ground almonds, 1 tablespoon white poppy seeds and 4 tablespoons korma curry paste and mix thoroughly. Add 150 ml (¼ pint) vegetable stock and 250 ml (8 fl oz) single cream. Stir until well combined. Bring to the boil, reduce the heat to low and simmer gently for 20–25 minutes, stirring often.

caribbean lamb stoba

Serves **4**
Preparation time **25 minutes**
Cooking time **1¾ hours**

2 tablespoons **sunflower oil**
750 g (1½ lb) **boneless leg
of lamb**, cut into bite-sized
cubes
2 **onions**, finely chopped
2 teaspoons finely grated
fresh **root ginger**
1 **scotch bonnet chilli**, thinly
sliced
1 **red pepper**, deseeded and
roughly chopped
2 teaspoons ground **allspice**
3 teaspoons ground **cumin**
1 **cinnamon stick**
pinch of grated **nutmeg**
400 g (13 oz) canned
chopped tomatoes
300 g (10 oz) **cherry
tomatoes**
finely grated rind and juice
of 2 **limes**
65 g (2½ oz) soft **brown
sugar**
200 g (7 oz) fresh or frozen
peas
salt and **pepper**

Heat half the oil in a large, heavy-based saucepan.
Brown the lamb, in batches, for 3–4 minutes. Remove
with a slotted spoon and set aside.

Heat the remaining oil in the saucepan and add the
onions, ginger, chilli, red pepper and spices. Stir-fry for
3–4 minutes and then add the lamb with the canned
and cherry tomatoes, lime rind and juice, and sugar.
Season and bring to the boil. Reduce the heat, cover
tightly and simmer gently for 1½ hours or until the
lamb is tender.

Stir in the peas 5 minutes before serving. To serve,
ladle onto warmed plates and eat with rice or Roti
(see page 222).

For Caribbean lamb, sweet potato & okra stoba,
add 500 g (1 lb) sweet potato, peeled and cubed,
after 30 minutes of cooking. Fry 250 g (8 oz) okra,
trimmed and thickly sliced, over a medium-high heat
for about 5 minutes, or until lightly browned but
still tender. Add the okra with the peas and finish
as above.

turkish lamb & spinach curry

Serves **4**
Preparation time **20 minutes**
Cooking time **2 hours**

4 tablespoons **sunflower oil**
600 g (1 lb 4 oz) **boneless
   shoulder of lamb**, cut into
   bite-sized pieces
1 **onion**, finely chopped
3 **garlic cloves**, crushed
1 teaspoon ground **ginger**
2 teaspoons ground **turmeric**
large pinch of grated **nutmeg**
4 tablespoons **sultanas**
1 teaspoon ground **cinnamon**
1 teaspoon **paprika**
400 g (13 oz) canned
   chopped tomatoes
300 ml (½ pint) **lamb stock**
400 g (13 oz) **baby leaf
   spinach**
salt and **pepper**

Heat half the oil in a large, heavy-based saucepan and brown the lamb, in batches, for 3–4 minutes. Remove with a slotted spoon and set aside.

Heat the remaining oil in the pan and add the onion, garlic, ginger, turmeric, nutmeg, sultanas, cinnamon and paprika. Stir-fry for 1–2 minutes and then add the lamb. Stir-fry for 2–3 minutes and then add the tomatoes and stock. Season well and bring to the boil. Reduce the heat, cover tightly and simmer very gently (using a heat diffuser if possible) for 1½ hours.

Add the spinach in batches until it is all wilted, cover and cook for a further 10–12 minutes, stirring occasionally. Remove from the heat and serve drizzled with whisked yogurt, if liked.

For Turkish lamb & aubergine curry, use a large aubergine instead of the spinach. Cut the aubergine into bite-sized chunks and fry it in oil until light golden brown, along with the lamb. You may need to add a little more oil to fry the aubergine.

kheema aloo

Serves **4**

Preparation time **10 minutes**

Cooking time **15–20 minutes**

1 tablespoon **vegetable oil**

4 **cardamom pods**

1 **cinnamon stick**

3 **cloves**

2 **onions**, finely chopped

375 g (12 oz) **minced lamb**

2 teaspoons **garam masala**

2 teaspoons **chilli powder**

2 **garlic cloves**, crushed

2 teaspoons grated fresh **root ginger**

2 teaspoons **salt**

200 g (7 oz) **potatoes**, cut into 1 cm (½ inch) cubes

200 g (7 oz) canned **chopped tomatoes**

100 ml (3½ fl oz) **hot water**

4 tablespoons chopped fresh **coriander**

Heat the oil in a nonstick frying pan and add the cardamom, cinnamon and cloves. Fry for 1 minute, then add the onions and fry, stirring, for 3–4 minutes.

Add the lamb to the pan with the garam masala, chilli powder, garlic, ginger and salt. Stir well to break up the mince and fry for 5–7 minutes.

Add the potatoes, tomatoes and the measured hot water, cover and simmer gently for 5–10 minutes or until the potatoes are tender.

Stir in the chopped coriander and serve hot with boiled rice or bread.

For kheema aloo with spinach & peas, add 250 g (8 oz) baby spinach leaves or shredded large spinach and 150 g (5 oz) frozen peas with the potatoes. Prepare the curry as above.

coconut lamb curry

Serves **4**

Preparation time **15 minutes**

Cooking time **about 2 hours**

2 tablespoons **sunflower oil**

1 **onion**, thinly sliced

2 teaspoons grated fresh **root ginger**

2 teaspoons crushed **garlic**

1 teaspoon ground **cinnamon**

20 **curry leaves**

2 tablespoons mild **curry powder**

1 tablespoon ground **coriander**

1 teaspoon ground **turmeric**

1 teaspoon **chilli powder**

625 g (1¼ lb) **boneless lamb**, cut into chunks

400 ml (14 fl oz) **coconut milk**

200 ml (7 fl oz) **vegetable stock**

100 g (3½ oz) fresh **coconut**, grated

6 tablespoons chopped fresh **coriander**

salt and **pepper**

Heat the oil in a large, heavy-based saucepan. Add the onion and stir-fry over a medium heat for 4–5 minutes. Stir in the ginger, garlic, cinnamon, curry leaves, curry powder, ground coriander, turmeric and chilli powder. Stir-fry for 2–3 minutes and then add the lamb.

Stir-fry for 2–3 minutes and then stir in the coconut milk and stock. Bring to the boil, season well and cover tightly. Cook over a very low heat (using a heat diffuser if possible), stirring occasionally, for 1½–2 hours or until the lamb is tender. Remove from the heat and sprinkle over the grated coconut and chopped fresh coriander before serving.

For coconut chicken curry, use 750 g (1½ lb) skinless chicken thighs on the bone, instead of the lamb, and reduce the cooking time to 1–1½ hours. After 1 hours cooking add ½ small cauliflower, cut into florets, and 250 g (8 oz) carrots, peeled, halved lengthways and sliced. Sprinkle in 50 g (2 oz) sultanas or raisins, if liked.

royal lamb biryani

Serves **4**

Preparation time **30 minutes**,
 plus marinating and standing

Cooking time **about 1½ hours**

4 **garlic** cloves, crushed

1 teaspoon finely grated fresh
 root ginger

150 ml (¼ pint) **natural yogurt**

6 tablespoons finely chopped
 fresh **coriander**

500 g (1 lb) **boneless lamb**,
 cut into bite-sized pieces

8 tablespoons **sunflower oil**

2 **onions**, finely chopped

2 tablespoons medium **curry
 powder**

200 g (7 oz) canned **chopped
 tomatoes**

2 teaspoons **cumin seeds**

6 **cloves**

10 **black peppercorns**

4 green **cardamom pods**

1 **cinnamon stick**

200 g (7 oz) **basmati rice**

400 ml (14 fl oz) **water**

1 teaspoon **saffron threads**

3 tablespoons warm **milk**

butter, for greasing

salt and **pepper**

Mix together the garlic, ginger, yogurt and fresh coriander and rub into the lamb. Marinate in the refrigerator for 4–6 hours. Heat half the oil in a heavy-based pan, add half the onions and cook for 12–15 minutes until golden. Add the meat and cook over a high heat for 15 minutes, stirring often.

Stir in the curry powder and tomatoes, season and bring to the boil. Reduce the heat and simmer for 30 minutes or until the lamb is tender. Set aside.

Meanwhile, heat the remaining oil in a separate pan. Add the cumin seeds, the remaining onion, cloves, peppercorns, cardamoms and cinnamon and stir-fry for 6–8 minutes. Add the rice and stir-fry for 2 minutes. Pour in the measured water, bring to the boil, cover and simmer for 6–7 minutes. Remove from the heat. Mix the saffron with the milk and set aside.

Lightly butter an ovenproof casserole dish. Spread a thin layer of the meat mixture over the base and cover evenly with half the rice. Drizzle over half the saffron mixture. Top with the remaining lamb then the remaining rice. Drizzle over the remaining saffron mixture and cover with foil and then the lid. Cook in a preheated oven at 180°C (350°F), Gas Mark 4, for 30 minutes.

Remove from the oven and allow to rest, still covered, for 30 minutes before serving.

minted rack of lamb

Serves **4**

Preparation time **20 minutes**, plus marinating

Cooking time **20–25 minutes**

4 French-trimmed **racks of lamb**, each with 4–5 ribs
100 g (3½ oz) **mint leaves**, finely chopped
50 g (2 oz) fresh **coriander**, finely chopped
2 teaspoons finely grated fresh **root ginger**
2 teaspoons crushed **garlic**
2 **red chillies**, finely chopped
4 tablespoons **sunflower oil**
1 tablespoon medium **curry paste**
4 tablespoons **lemon juice**
4 tablespoons **coconut cream**
1 teaspoon **sugar**

Prick the flesh of the racks of lamb all over with a sharp knife. Place them in a shallow, non-metallic dish and set aside.

Place all the remaining ingredients in a food processor and process until you have a fairly smooth paste. Rub this paste all over the racks of lamb, cover and marinate in the refrigerator for 24 hours.

When ready to cook, allow the lamb to come to room temperature. Place the racks on a baking sheet lined with nonstick baking paper, flesh side up, and cook in a preheated oven at 180°C (350°F), Gas Mark 4 for 20–25 minutes or until cooked to your liking.

Remove from the oven and cover with foil. Allow to rest for 5–6 minutes before serving.

For minted chicken kebabs, replace the racks of lamb with 750 g (1½ lb) skinned and boned chicken cut in to bite-sized pieces. Marinate for 6–8 hours, or overnight if time permits. Thread the chicken pieces between 8 metal skewers and cook under a medium-hot grill for 5–6 minutes on each side, or until cooked through.

parsi dansak

Serves **4**
Preparation time **30 minutes**
Cooking time **1¼–1¾ hours**

750 g (1½ lb) **boneless lamb shoulder**, cut into large chunks
3 tablespoons **red lentils**
3 tablespoons **yellow split peas**
3 tablespoons **whole green lentils**
300 g (10 oz) **pumpkin**, roughly chopped
200 g (7 oz) **potatoes**, chopped
1 teaspoon ground **turmeric**
4 tablespoons **sunflower oil**
2 large **onions**, halved and thinly sliced
1 teaspoon finely grated fresh **root ginger**
3 teaspoons crushed **garlic**
3 tablespoons **medium curry powder**
2 teaspoons **tamarind paste**
2 teaspoons grated **palm sugar**
salt and **pepper**
fresh **coriander**, to garnish

Place the meat, lentils, split peas, pumpkin, potatoes and turmeric in a large, heavy-based saucepan. Season well and pour in enough water to cover. Bring to the boil, reduce the heat and simmer gently for 1–1½ hours or until the meat is tender. Remove the meat from this mixture and set aside. Use a hand-held electric mixer to purée the vegetable mixture until fairly smooth. Return the meat to the pan and set aside.

Meanwhile, heat 3 tablespoons of the oil in a large frying pan and stir-fry the onions over a gentle heat for 15–20 minutes or until golden brown. Reserve half the onions and add the rest to the meat mixture.

Heat the remaining oil in the frying pan and fry the ginger, garlic and curry powder over a medium heat for 2–3 minutes. Stir this mixture into the meat curry, along with the tamarind and sugar. Stir to mix well and simmer the curry for 10–15 minutes.

Remove from the heat and serve immediately, garnished with the reserved onions and coriander leaves. Serve with yellow basmati rice or a rice dish such as Carrot & Pea Pilaf (see page 220), mango chutney and crispy pappadoms.

For lamb & mixed vegetable curry, use 250 g (8 oz) each of butternut squash, carrots, parsnips and celeriac instead of pumpkin and potatoes. Cut the vegetables into even-sized pieces. Prepare this curry as above.

malaysian rendang lamb

Serves **4**

Preparation time **15 minutes**

Cooking time **2¾ hours**

2 tablespoons **sunflower oil**

1 kg (2 lb) **leg of lamb**, butterflied

2 **onions**, finely chopped

1 tablespoon ground **coriander**

1 teaspoon ground **turmeric**

6 **garlic cloves**, crushed

6 tablespoons very finely chopped **lemon grass**

4–6 **bird's eye chillies**, chopped

4 tablespoons finely chopped fresh **coriander root** and **stem**

400 ml (14 fl oz) **coconut milk**

salt and **pepper**

Heat the oil in a deep, heavy-based casserole dish and brown the lamb on both sides for about 5–6 minutes.

Place the remaining ingredients in a food processor and blend until smooth. Season well.

Pour this mixture over the lamb and bring to the boil. Cover tightly and cook in a preheated oven at 150°C (300°F), Gas Mark 2, turning the lamb occasionally, for 2½ hours or until the lamb is meltingly tender and most of the liquid has evaporated.

Remove from the oven and allow to stand for 10–12 minutes before serving, cut into thick slices.

For winter salad, to serve as an accompaniment to this dish, mix together 300 g (10 oz) green cabbage, finely shredded, 1 carrot, coarsely grated and 1 red onion, finely sliced. In a separate dish mix together 3 tablespoons light olive oil and the juice of 1 lemon. Season the dressing well and pour over the salad mixture. Toss until the salad is thoroughly coated in the dressing and serve.

lamb rogan josh

Serves **4**

Preparation time **20 minutes**

Cooking time **about 3 hours**

2 tablespoons **sunflower oil**

625 g (1¼ lb) **boneless lamb**, cut into large chunks

2 large **onions**, thickly sliced

3 **garlic cloves**, crushed

2 teaspoons finely grated fresh **root ginger**

2 **cinnamon sticks**

6 green **cardamom pods**

4 tablespoons **medium curry paste**

400 g (13 oz) canned **chopped tomatoes**

6 tablespoons **tomato purée**

1 teaspoon **sugar**

400 ml (14 fl oz) **lamb stock**

4 **potatoes**, cut into chunks

salt and **pepper**

chopped fresh **coriander**, to garnish

Heat half the oil in a large, heavy-based casserole dish and cook the lamb, in batches, for 3–4 minutes until browned, then remove with a slotted spoon and set aside.

Add the remaining oil to the dish and add the onions. Cook over a medium heat for 10–12 minutes, stirring often, until soft and lightly browned.

Add the garlic, ginger, cinnamon and cardamom pods. Stir-fry for 1–2 minutes and then add the curry paste and lamb. Stir-fry for 2–3 minutes and then stir in the tomatoes, tomato purée, sugar, stock and potatoes. Season well and bring to the boil.

Reduce the heat, cover and simmer very gently (using a heat diffuser if possible) for 2–2½ hours or until the lamb is tender. Remove from the heat and serve garnished with chopped fresh coriander and drizzled with yogurt, if liked.

For baked lamb curry on the hob, once you have added the tomatoes and potatoes, transfer the dish to a preheated oven at 140°C (275°F), Gas Mark 1 and cook for about 3 hours.

For baked spicy aubergine & courgettes, to serve as an accompaniment, mix 1 diced aubergine with 2 diced courgettes. Toss with 2 tablespoons garam masala and 4 tablespoons sunflower oil. Place in an ovenproof dish and bake for 45 minutes, turning occasionally, or until tender.

kashmiri lamb curry

Serves **4**

Preparation time **20 minutes**, plus marinating

Cooking time **about 2¼ hours**

750 g (1½ lb) **lamb neck fillet**, cut into bite-sized pieces

150 ml (¼ pint) **natural yogurt**, lightly whisked

150 ml (¼ pint) **single cream**

1 tablespoon crushed **garlic**

2 teaspoons finely grated fresh **root ginger**

2 teaspoons **chilli powder**

1 tablespoon ground **coriander**

1 teaspoon ground **turmeric**

2 tablespoons **sunflower oil**

1 tablespoon **fennel seeds**, crushed

2 **onions**, sliced

2 **tomatoes**, roughly chopped

1 dried **bay leaf**

300 ml (½ pint) **lamb stock**

salt and **pepper**

chopped fresh **coriander**, to garnish

Place the lamb in a large, non-metallic bowl. Mix together the yogurt, cream, garlic, ginger, chilli powder, ground coriander and turmeric. Season well and pour this mixture over the lamb. Toss to mix well, cover and marinate in the refrigerator for 24 hours.

Allow the lamb to come to room temperature before cooking. Heat the oil in a heavy-based casserole dish, then add the fennel seeds and onions. Stir-fry for 3–4 minutes and then turn the heat to high.

Add the lamb mixture and stir-fry for 3–4 minutes. Stir in the tomatoes, bay leaf and stock, bring to the boil and remove from the heat. Stir well to combine, cover tightly and cook in a preheated oven at 150°C (300°F), Gas Mark 2, stirring occasionally, for 2 hours or until the lamb is tender. Stir vigorously to mix well and serve immediately with naan, garnished with fresh coriander.

For fruity Kashmiri chicken curry, omit the tomatoes and add 100 g (3½ oz) dried apricots, halved, and 2 firm pears, peeled, cored and diced, with the stock.

marinated lamb chops

Serves **4**

Preparation time **10 minutes**, plus marinating

Cooking time **25–30 minutes**

3 **garlic cloves**, crushed

1 teaspoon finely grated fresh **root ginger**

finely grated rind and juice of 2 **lemons**

1 tablespoon ground **cumin**

3 tablespoons **tandoori curry paste**

250 g (8 oz) **natural yogurt**

8 **lamb loin chops** or **cutlets**

salt and **pepper**

To garnish

chopped **mint** leaves

lime wedges

Mix together the garlic, ginger, lemon rind and juice, cumin, curry paste and yogurt in a bowl. Season well. Place the lamb in a shallow, non-metallic bowl in a single layer. Pour the yogurt mixture over the lamb and toss to coat well. Cover and leave to marinate in the refrigerator for 24–48 hours.

Place the marinated lamb on a baking sheet lined with nonstick baking paper and cook in a preheated oven at 200°C (400°F), Gas Mark 6 for 25–30 minutes or until cooked to your liking.

Serve immediately, garnished with chopped mint and lime wedges.

For lamb kebabs, use 500 g (1 lb) large chunks of boneless lamb, such as leg or shoulder, and marinate the meat before threading it on skewers. Do not stint on the marinating time, as the yogurt mixture tenderizes the meat. Cook the kebabs under a preheated hot grill for 4–5 minutes on each side.

fish and seafood

spiced halibut curry

Serves **4**

Preparation time **15 minutes**, plus chilling

Cooking time **40–50 minutes**

60 ml (2½ fl oz) **lemon juice**

60 ml (2½ fl oz) **rice wine vinegar**

2 tablespoons **cumin seeds**

1 teaspoon **chilli powder**

1 teaspoon ground **turmeric**

1 teaspoon **salt**

750 g (1½ lb) thick **halibut fillets**, skinned and cut into cubes

4 tablespoons **sunflower oil**

1 **onion**, finely chopped

3 **garlic cloves**, crushed

2 tablespoons finely grated fresh **root ginger**

2 teaspoons **black mustard seeds**

2 x 400 g (13 oz) cans **chopped tomatoes**

1 teaspoon **sugar**

To garnish

chopped fresh **coriander**

sliced **green chillies**

natural yogurt (optional)

Mix together the lemon juice, vinegar, cumin, chilli powder, turmeric and salt in a shallow glass bowl. Add the fish and turn to coat evenly. Cover and chill for 25–30 minutes.

Meanwhile, heat a wok over a high heat and add the oil. When hot, add the onion, garlic, ginger and mustard seeds. Reduce the heat and cook gently for 10 minutes, stirring occasionally.

Add the tomatoes and sugar, bring to the boil, reduce the heat, cover and cook gently for 15–20 minutes, stirring occasionally.

Add the fish and its marinade, stir gently to mix and then cover and simmer gently for 15–20 minutes or until the fish is cooked through and flakes easily.

Garnish with chopped fresh coriander and green chillies and drizzle over some natural yogurt, if desired. Serve with steamed basmati rice, pickles and pappadoms.

For dry-spiced haddock, use 750 g (1½ lb) haddock fillets instead of halibut, cutting the fillets into large chunks. Heat a wok over a high heat and pour in the sunflower oil. When hot, add the onion, garlic, fresh root ginger and black mustard seeds. Add the fish and cook for 5 minutes until just firm, turning occasionally. Add 2–3 tablespoons water and cook for 3–5 minutes. Serve drizzled with yogurt and sprinkled with coriander.

salmon in banana leaves

Serves **4**
Preparation time **15 minutes**
Cooking time **15 minutes**

large bunch of fresh
  coriander, roughly chopped
3 tablespoons chopped
  mint leaves
2 **garlic cloves**, crushed
1 teaspoon grated fresh **root
  ginger**
4 **red chillies**, deseeded and
  chopped
2 teaspoons ground **cumin**
1 teaspoon ground **coriander**
2 teaspoons soft **brown sugar**
2 tablespoons **lime juice**
150 ml (¼ pint) **coconut milk**
4 thick **salmon fillets**, skinned
4 squares of **banana leaf**
  (about 30 cm (12 inches)
  square)
salt and **pepper**

Put the fresh coriander, mint, garlic, ginger, chillies,
cumin, ground coriander, sugar, lime juice and coconut
milk into a food processor or blender and blend until
fairly smooth. Season and set aside.

Place each salmon fillet on a square of banana leaf
and spoon some of the herb and spice mixture over it.
Carefully wrap the fish in the leaf to make a neat
parcel and secure with wooden skewers. If the banana
leaves are difficult to handle, dip them in boiling water
for 15–20 seconds and they will become more supple.

Place the parcels on a large baking sheet and bake in
a preheated oven at 200°C (400°F), Gas Mark 6 for
15 minutes.

Remove the parcels from the oven, place on a serving
plate and open the packages at the table.

For swordfish parcels, make the parcels from baking
paper or foil instead of banana leaves. Use 4 x 175 g
(6 oz) portions swordfish instead of salmon. Prepare
as above and bake in a preheated over at 180°C
(350°F), Gas Mark 4, for 20–25 minutes. Serve with
a moist accompaniment of yogurt with chopped
coriander and diced tomato.

malaysian scallop & prawn curry

Serves **4**
Preparation time **20 minutes**
Cooking time **20–25 minutes**

1 tablespoon **chilli powder**
1 teaspoon ground **coriander**
2 teaspoons ground **cumin**
2 **garlic cloves**, crushed
1 **onion**, finely chopped
6 tablespoons finely chopped
　lemon grass
1 teaspoon grated **galangal** or
　fresh **root ginger**
1 tablespoon grated **palm**
　sugar
½ teaspoon **shrimp paste**
2 tablespoons finely chopped
　unroasted peanuts
600 ml (1 pint) **coconut milk**
200 g (7 oz) **green beans**,
　trimmed and halved
500 g (1 lb) raw **tiger prawns**
500 g (1 lb) raw **scallops**

To garnish
Thai basil leaves
chopped **roasted peanuts**
chopped **red chillies**

Place the chilli powder, ground coriander, cumin, garlic, onion, lemon grass, galangal or ginger, palm sugar, shrimp paste, peanuts and coconut milk in a food processor and process until fairly smooth.

Place a large wok over a high heat and add the spice mixture. Bring to the boil, reduce the heat and simmer gently, uncovered, for 12–15 minutes, stirring occasionally.

Add the green beans, prawns and scallops and bring back to the boil. Reduce the heat and simmer gently for 6–8 minutes or until the prawns and scallops are cooked through.

Remove from the heat and scatter over some Thai basil leaves, chopped roasted peanuts and sliced red chilli before serving.

For spicy squid & prawns, add 350 g (11½ oz) squid rings instead of the scallops and proceed as above. Serve with rice sticks or cellophane noodles instead of rice.

crab malabar-hill

Serves **4**
Preparation time **10 minutes**
Cooking time **5–6 minutes**

2 tablespoons **vegetable oil**
3 **garlic cloves**, finely
  chopped
2 teaspoons finely chopped
  fresh **root ginger**
6 **spring onions**, very thinly
  sliced
3 **red chillies**, deseeded and
  finely sliced
625 g (1 ¼ lb) fresh **white**
  crab meat
grated rind and juice of
  1 **lime**
4 tablespoons chopped fresh
  coriander
2 tablespoons chopped **mint**
  leaves
salt and **pepper**
crisp **lettuce** leaves, to serve

Heat the oil in a large wok or nonstick frying pan and add the garlic, ginger, spring onions and chillies. Fry, stirring constantly, for 2–3 minutes.

Add the crab meat, lime rind and juice, coriander and mint. Stir-fry for 2–3 minutes, season with salt and pepper and serve hot on crisp lettuce leaves.

For spicy crab omelettes, use this spicy, tangy crab mixture as the filling. Make 4 thin omelettes, using 2 eggs each, in a nonstick frying pan. Divide the crab mixture between them and fold over to enclose it. Serve with a crisp green salad.

achaari prawns

Serves **4**
Preparation time **20 minutes**
Cooking time **about 40 minutes**

4 tablespoons **sunflower oil**
8 **shallots**, finely chopped
6–8 **curry leaves**
1 tablespoon finely grated fresh **root ginger**
1 tablespoon crushed **garlic**
3 **red chillies**, halved lengthways
1 tablespoon ground **coriander**
3 teaspoons **cumin seeds**
3 teaspoons **black mustard seeds**
3 teaspoons **nigella seeds**
3 teaspoons **fennel seeds**
400 g (13 oz) canned **chopped tomatoes**
750 g (1½ lb) raw **tiger prawns**, peeled and deveined, tails left on
6 tablespoons finely chopped fresh **coriander**
salt and **pepper**

Heat the oil in a large, nonstick wok or frying pan and add the shallots. Stir-fry over a medium heat for 10 minutes until lightly golden.

Add the curry leaves, ginger, garlic and chillies. Stir-fry for 1 minute and then add the ground coriander, cumin, mustard, nigella and fennel seeds. Season well and stir-fry for 1–2 minutes.

Stir in the tomatoes and bring the sauce to the boil. Reduce the heat and cook gently for 20–25 minutes, stirring occasionally.

Add the prawns to the pan and cook over a high heat for 3–4 minutes or until the prawns turn pink and are cooked through. Remove from the heat, stir in the chopped fresh coriander and serve immediately with rice.

For spiced prawn chapatis, use peeled cooked prawns instead of tiger prawns, thawed if frozen. Add 4 tomatoes, chopped, instead of canned tomatoes, and cook for 5 minutes, until hot. Meanwhile, warm 8 chapatis in a preheated oven at 150°C (300°F), Gas Mark 2. Add the coriander to the prawn curry, then divide among the chapatis and roll up. Serve immediately.

spiced mussel curry

Serves **4**
Preparation time **10 minutes**
Cooking time **10–12 minutes**

1 kg (2 lb) live **mussels**
1 tablespoon **vegetable oil**
1 **onion**, finely chopped
4 **garlic cloves**, crushed
3 **green chillies**, finely
  chopped
1 teaspoon ground **turmeric**
100 ml (3½ fl oz) **white wine
  vinegar**
400 ml (14 fl oz) **coconut
  milk**
2 teaspoons **sugar**
4 tablespoons chopped fresh
  coriander
salt and **pepper**
grated fresh **coconut**,
  to garnish

Rinse the mussels under cold running water and
scrape off any beards. Discard any that are open
or that do not close when sharply tapped. Drain and
set aside.

Heat the oil in a large saucepan, add the onion, garlic,
chillies and turmeric and fry for 2–3 minutes. Add the
mussels, vinegar, coconut milk, sugar and coriander.
Stir well and bring to the boil.

Cover and cook gently for 5–6 minutes or until all the
mussels have opened. Discard any that remain shut.

Transfer the mussels to a serving bowl with a slotted
spoon, season the cooking juices and pour over the
mussels. Garnish with grated coconut and serve with
crusty white bread to mop up the juices.

For sweet & sour mussel curry, add half a pineapple,
woody sections of core removed and the flesh cut
into bite-sized chunks. Add to the curry at the same
time as the mussels and proceed as above.

yellow cod & potato curry

Serves **4**
Preparation time **15 minutes**
Cooking time **25 minutes**

3 **garlic cloves**, crushed
2 **green chillies**, deseeded
  and finely chopped
2 teaspoons finely grated
  fresh **root ginger**
2 tablespoons **sunflower oil**
1 **onion**, finely chopped
1 tablespoon ground **turmeric**
200 ml (7 fl oz) **coconut milk**
200 ml (7 fl oz) **water**
2 **potatoes**, cut into small
  bite-sized pieces
750 g (1½ lb) thick **cod fillet**,
  skinned and cut into large
  bite-sized pieces
2 **tomatoes**, roughly chopped
salt
chopped fresh **coriander**,
  to garnish

Pound the garlic, chillies and ginger in a small mortar with a pestle until you have a smooth paste.

Heat the oil in a large nonstick wok or saucepan and add the garlic and chilli mixture. Stir-fry for 2–3 minutes, then add the onion and turmeric. Stir-fry for a further 2–3 minutes, then stir in the coconut milk, measured water and potatoes.

Bring to the boil, reduce the heat and simmer gently for 10–12 minutes, stirring occasionally.

Season the fish with salt and add to the pan with the tomatoes. Bring the mixture back to the boil, reduce the heat and simmer gently for 6–8 minutes or until the fish is cooked through. Garnish with chopped fresh coriander just before serving.

For chicken & baby new potato curry, use 4 boneless, skinless chicken breasts and cut them into bite-sized chunks. Use 400 g (13 oz) baby new potatoes, keeping them whole, and add the chicken to the curry at the same time as the potatoes.

southern-indian prawns

Serves **4**
Preparation time **10 minutes**
Cooking time **12–15 minutes**

1 tablespoon **sunflower oil**
2 **onions**, thinly sliced
8–10 **curry leaves**
1 teaspoon **nigella seeds**
1 **red chilli**, finely sliced
625 g (1¼ lb) raw **tiger
 prawns**, peeled and
 deveined
2 teaspoons grated fresh **root
 ginger**
2 teaspoons **salt**
1 tablespoon **fenugreek
 leaves**
1 tablespoon **lemon juice**

Heat the oil in a large, nonstick frying pan, add the onions, curry leaves and nigella seeds and stir-fry for 3 minutes.

Add the chilli and prawns and fry, stirring constantly, for 5–7 minutes. Add the ginger and salt and fry, stirring, for another minute or until the prawns turn pink and are just cooked through.

Finally, add the fenugreek leaves and lemon juice and cook for 1–2 minutes. Remove from the heat and serve hot with warmed white bread.

For spicy prawn salad, prepare the prawns and transfer to a dish. In a separate bowl mix together ½ iceberg lettuce, finely shredded, and 2 spring onions, diced. Divide the lettuce mix among four plates, then top with the prawns. Drizzle over a dressing made from 4 tablespoons mayonnaise and 4 tablespoons yogurt mixed with the grated rind of 1 lemon.

whole pomfret in banana leaf

Serves **4**

Preparation time **20 minutes**

Cooking time **15–20 minutes**

1 large **pomfret**, gutted and
cleaned

1 **banana leaf**, large enough
to wrap the fish in

5 cm (2 inch) piece of fresh
root ginger, peeled and cut
into matchsticks

50 ml (2 fl oz) **coconut cream**

6 tablespoons chopped fresh
coriander

6 tablespoons chopped **mint**

6 tablespoons **lime juice**

3 **spring onions**, finely sliced

4 **lime leaves**, finely shredded

2 **red chillies**, deseeded and
finely sliced

salt and **pepper**

Use a small sharp knife to score the fish flesh
diagonally on both sides. Dip the banana leaf into
boiling water for 15–20 seconds to make it supple
and pliable for wrapping the fish. Remove and rinse
under cold water. Dry with kitchen paper.

Mix together the ginger, coconut cream, chopped
herbs, lime juice, spring onions, lime leaves and chilli
in a bowl. Season the mixture to taste.

Lay the banana leaf on a work surface and place the
pomfret in the centre. Spread the herb mixture over
the pomfret and wrap in the leaf to form a neat parcel.
Secure with bamboo skewers or cocktail sticks.

Place the parcel in a large bamboo steamer and
steam, covered, over a wok of simmering water for
15–20 minutes or until the fish is cooked through.
Serve the fish immediately with steamed rice and
steamed Asian greens.

For stuffed spicy trout, divide the herb mix among
4 cleaned trout, placing it in the body cavities. Allow
to marinate for 30 minutes, then bake in an ovenproof
dish at 190°C (375°F), Gas Mark 5, for about
30 minutes, until cooked and aromatic.

ceylonese crab curry

Serves **4**
Preparation time **15 minutes**
Cooking time **25–35 minutes**

1 tablespoon **sunflower oil**
1 large **onion**, finely chopped
3 **garlic cloves**, finely chopped
1 teaspoon finely grated fresh **root ginger**
1 **red chilli**, finely chopped
10 **curry leaves**
1 tablespoon medium or hot **curry powder**
2 teaspoons ground **cinnamon**
1 teaspoon ground **turmeric**
400 ml (14 fl oz) **coconut milk**
200 ml (7 fl oz) **fish stock**
4 small soft shell **crabs**
4 tablespoons **lemon juice**
salt
lemon segments, for squeezing

Heat the oil in a large, nonstick wok and add the onion, garlic, ginger and chilli. Stir-fry for 1–2 minutes and add the curry leaves, curry powder, ground cinnamon and turmeric.

Stir-fry for 2–3 minutes and then add the coconut milk and stock. Bring to the boil, reduce the heat and simmer for 10–15 minutes, stirring occasionally.

Add the crab to the wok and simmer, covered, for 10–15 minutes. Remove from the heat and stir in the lemon juice. Season with salt and serve immediately with lemon segments, for squeezing.

For Ceylonese crabmeat curry, use 2 small or medium cooked crabs instead of soft shell crabs. Lift off the back shell of each crab and remove and discard the gills and stomach sac. Separate the claws from the bodies. Scoop out all the meat from the shells and body cavities, then crack the claws and remove the meat. Add the meat to the curry, and simmer gently for 4–5 minutes, until hot. Finish as above.

monkfish kebabs

Serves **4**
Preparation time **10 minutes**,
  plus marinating
Cooking time **8–10 minutes**

1 kg (2 lb) **monkfish fillet**, cut
  into 4 cm (1½ inch) cubes
200 g (7 oz) **natural yogurt**
4 tablespoons **lemon juice**
3 **garlic cloves**, crushed
2 teaspoons grated fresh **root
  ginger**
1 teaspoon hot **chilli powder**
1 teaspoon ground **cumin**
1 teaspoon ground **coriander**
2 **red chillies**, finely sliced
salt and **pepper**

To garnish
chopped fresh **coriander**
lime slices
sliced **red chillies**

Put the monkfish cubes into a non-metallic bowl. In a small bowl, mix together the yogurt, lemon juice, garlic, ginger, chilli powder, cumin, ground coriander and chillies and season with salt and pepper. Pour this over the fish, cover and marinate in the refrigerator overnight, if time allows.

Lift the fish out of the marinade and thread on to 8 flat metal skewers. Place on a grill rack and cook under a preheated hot grill for 8–10 minutes, turning once, until the fish is cooked through. Serve hot, garnished with chopped fresh coriander, lime slices and chilli slices.

For tandoori whiting fillets, make a marinade using 200 g (7 oz) natural yogurt, 4 tablespoons lemon juice, 2 garlic cloves, crushed, 1 teaspoon grated fresh root ginger and 1 teaspoon ground coriander. Place 4 whiting fillets in a non-metallic dish and pour over the marinade. Marinate the fish in the tandoori mixture overnight and cook as above.

kerala prawn curry

Serves **4**
Preparation time **15 minutes**
Cooking time **6–8 minutes**

2 tablespoons **sunflower oil**
3 **garlic cloves**, finely
  chopped
16 large raw **tiger prawns**,
  peeled and deveined
1 teaspoon finely grated fresh
  root ginger
1 **red chilli**, finely sliced
150 ml (¼ pint) **water**
100 ml (3½ fl oz) **coconut
  cream**
6 tablespoons finely chopped
  fresh **coriander**
salt
lime wedges, to garnish

Tamarind mixture
1 teaspoon **tamarind paste**
1 teaspoon hot **chilli powder**
2 teaspoons ground **cumin**
1 teaspoon ground **turmeric**
4 tablespoons **water**

To make the tamarind mixture, place the tamarind paste, chilli powder, cumin and turmeric in a small bowl with the measured water and stir to mix well.

Heat the oil in a large nonstick wok or frying pan over a medium heat. Add the garlic and prawns and stir-fry for 2–3 minutes.

Stir in the ginger, chilli, measured water and tamarind mixture. Bring to the boil, reduce the heat and simmer for 2 minutes, then stir in the coconut cream.

Gently simmer the mixture for 2–3 minutes, stirring constantly, until the prawns turn pink and are just cooked through.

Remove from the heat, season with salt and stir in the fresh coriander. Serve immediately with steamed basmati rice and pappadoms and garnished with lime wedges.

For Kerala mackerel curry, use 8 fresh mackerel fillets instead of the prawns. Simmer the fillets for 5 minutes until firm and cooked. Serve sprinkled with coriander and lime rind.

goan prawn curry

Serves **4**
Preparation time **15 minutes**
Cooking time **15 minutes**

1 teaspoon **chilli powder**
1 tablespoon **paprika**
½ teaspoon ground **turmeric**
4 **garlic cloves**, crushed
2 teaspoons grated fresh **root ginger**
2 tablespoons ground **coriander**
1 teaspoon ground **cumin**
2 teaspoons soft **brown sugar**
300 ml (½ pint) **water**
400 ml (14 fl oz) **coconut milk**
2 teaspoons **salt**
1 tablespoon **tamarind paste**
625 g (1¼ lb) raw **tiger prawns**

Put the chilli powder, paprika, turmeric, garlic, ginger, coriander, cumin, sugar and measured water into a bowl. Mix well and transfer to a large saucepan. Bring this mixture to the boil, then reduce the heat, cover and simmer gently for 7–8 minutes.

Add the coconut milk, salt and tamarind paste and bring to a simmer.

Stir in the prawns and cook briskly until they turn pink and are just cooked through. Serve hot, accompanied by boiled white rice.

For prawns with spinach & egg, hard boil 8 eggs, shell and cut in half. Add 250 g (8 oz) baby leaf spinach to the coconut curry sauce and simmer for 3 minutes. Add 450 g (14½ oz) fresh cooked prawns and cook for 2 minutes. Add the eggs and cook for a further 2 minutes. Serve with boiled white rice.

spiced fish brochettes

Serves **4**
Preparation time **20 minutes**
Cooking time **5–6 minutes**

4 **trout fillets**, skinned
½ teaspoon ground **turmeric**
1 tablespoon **mild curry paste**
8 tablespoons **lemon juice**
1 tablespoon **sunflower oil**
3 tablespoons **chilli-roasted peanuts**, roughly chopped
salt

Noodles
300 g (10 oz) **rice noodles**
1 tablespoon **sunflower oil**
1 red **chilli**, deseeded and finely sliced
4 **spring onions**, cut into slivers
4 tablespoons roughly chopped **mint**
4 tablespoons roughly chopped **Thai basil**

To garnish
chopped **mint**
finely sliced **red chilli**

Place the trout fillets in a large mixing bowl. Mix together the turmeric, curry paste, lemon juice and oil and pour over the fish. Season and toss to mix well.

Place the rice noodles in a bowl and pour over boiling water to cover. Leave to soak for 3–4 minutes and then drain. Refresh in cold water, drain and set aside.

Thread 2 bamboo skewers through each trout fillet and place on a heatproof plate in a bamboo steamer. Cover and place over a wok of simmering water (making sure the water doesn't touch the steamer) and steam for 5–6 minutes or until the fish is just cooked through.

Meanwhile, heat the oil in a wok add the chilli, spring onions and drained noodles. Stir-fry over high heat for 2–3 minutes and then stir in the chopped herbs. Season and divide among 4 warmed plates or shallow bowls. Top each serving with a steamed fish brochette and scatter over the chopped chilli-roasted peanuts. Garnish with chopped mint and finely sliced red chilli and serve immediately.

For mint & coriander herb salad, to serve as an accompaniment, place 65 g (2½ oz) each of fresh coriander and mint leaves with 50 g (2 oz) baby mixed salad leaves in a mixing bowl. Pour over a well-seasoned dressing of 2 tablespoons red wine vinegar, 4 tablespoons olive oil and 1 teaspoon Dijon mustard. Mix well and serve.

creamy prawn curry

Serves **4**
Preparation time **10 minutes**
Cooking time **10–13 minutes**

2 tablespoons **vegetable oil**
1 **onion**, finely sliced
2 **garlic cloves**, finely sliced
2 tablespoons finely chopped
  fresh **root ginger**
1 tablespoon ground
  coriander
1 tablespoon ground **cumin**
½ teaspoon ground **turmeric**
200 ml (7 fl oz) **coconut milk**
125 ml (4 fl oz) **vegetable
  stock**
600 g (1 lb 3 oz) raw **tiger
  prawns**, peeled and
  deveined
grated rind and juice of
  1 **lime**
4 tablespoons finely chopped
  fresh **coriander**
salt and **pepper**

Heat the oil in a nonstick wok or frying pan and fry the onion, garlic and ginger for 4–5 minutes. Add the ground coriander, cumin and turmeric and stir-fry for a further 1 minute.

Pour in the coconut milk and stock and bring to the boil. Reduce the heat and simmer for 2–3 minutes. Stir in the prawns, lime rind and juice, then simmer for 3–4 minutes or until the prawns are pink and cooked through.

Stir in the chopped fresh coriander and season the curry well. Serve at once, with steamed basmati or jasmine rice.

For prawn & spinach curry paratha, defrost 125 g (4 oz) frozen whole-leaf spinach and stir into the curry with the prawns. You may need to heat the curry for another minute or two to make sure the prawns are cooked. Heat 4 paratha under the grill following the packet instructions and serve as a base for the curry.

coconut clam curry

Serves **4**

Preparation time **25 minutes**

Cooking time **10 minutes**

1 tablespoon **sunflower oil**

6 **garlic cloves**, roughly chopped

1 tablespoon finely chopped fresh **root ginger**

3–4 large **red chillies**, split in half lengthways

6 **spring onions**, finely chopped

400 ml (14 fl oz) **coconut milk**

2 **lemon grass** stalks, halved lengthways

3 tablespoons **light soy sauce**

finely grated rind and juice of 2 **limes**

1 teaspoon **caster sugar**

1.5 kg (3 lb) live **clams**, scrubbed

large handful of chopped fresh **coriander**

salt and **pepper**

Heat a nonstick wok or large saucepan over a high heat and then add the oil. Stir in the garlic, ginger, red chillies and spring onions. Stir-fry for 30 seconds and then add the coconut milk, lemon grass, soy sauce, lime rind and juice, and sugar. Bring to the boil then add the clams.

Bring back to the boil, cover and cook briskly for 3–5 minutes or until all the clams have opened. Discard any that remain closed.

Remove from the heat, stir in the coriander and season well. Ladle into warmed bowls and serve immediately with a spoon for the juices.

For coconut mussel curry, prepare 1.5 kg (3 lb) mussels. Scrub and debeard them discarding any that are open or do not close when tapped. Add as above but cook them for 5–6 minutes. Discard any that do not open. Serve with French bread to mop up the fragrant juices.

thai fishball curry

Serves **4**
Preparation time **15 minutes**
Cooking time **15–20 minutes**

1 tablespoon **sunflower oil**
100 g (3½ oz) **Thai red curry paste**
2 x 400 ml (14 fl oz) cans **coconut milk**
500 g (1 lb) **fishballs**
2 teaspoons finely grated **palm sugar**
4 **lime leaves**, finely shredded
1 tablespoon very finely chopped **lemon grass**
2 teaspoons **Thai fish sauce**
150 g (5 oz) **bean sprouts**

To garnish
sliced **red chilli**
chopped fresh **coriander**

Heat the oil in a large nonstick wok and add the curry paste. Stir-fry for 1–2 minutes and then add the coconut milk. Bring to the boil, reduce the heat and simmer gently, uncovered, for 6–8 minutes.

Add the fishballs, palm sugar, lime leaves, lemon grass, fish sauce and bean sprouts. Bring to the boil, reduce the heat again and simmer, uncovered, for a further 6–8 minutes.

To serve, ladle the curry into bowls, garnish with sliced red chilli and fresh coriander and serve with steamed jasmine rice.

For homemade fishballs, blend together 750 g (1½ lb) firm white fish fillet, 2 crushed garlic cloves, 2 tablespoons cornflour, 2 tablespoons dark soy sauce, 2 tablespoons chopped fresh coriander root and 1 teaspoon grated fresh root ginger. Roll the mixture into small bite-sized balls and use as directed in the recipe.

vegetarian

okra & coconut curry

Serves **4**

Preparation time **15 minutes**

Cooking time **10–12 minutes**

625 g (1 ¼ lb) **okra**

4 tablespoons **sunflower oil**

1 **onion**, finely chopped

1 tablespoon **mustard seeds**

1 tablespoon **cumin seeds**

2–3 dried **red chilles**

10–12 **curry leaves**

½ teaspoon ground **turmeric**

100 g (3½ oz) grated fresh
  coconut

salt

First prepare the okra by cutting them diagonally into 1.5 cm (¾ inch) lengths. Set aside.

Heat the oil in a nonstick wok or frying pan, add the onion and stir-fry over a medium heat for 5–6 minutes until softened.

Add the mustard seeds, cumin seeds, red chillies and curry leaves and stir-fry over a high heat for 2 minutes.

Stir in the okra and turmeric and continue to stir-fry over a high heat for 3–4 minutes.

Remove from the heat, sprinkle over the coconut and season well. Serve immediately with steamed rice, Parathas (see page 226) or crispy pappadoms.

For crispy okra, roast the mustard and cumin seeds in a small dry pan until they pop, then place in a dish and set aside. Cut the okra into thin slices and toss with 1 teaspoon ground turmeric, then deep-fry for 1–2 minutes until crisp and golden. Drain the okra on kitchen paper, sprinkle with salt, then toss with the roasted seeds. Serve in a bowl with fresh coconut shavings.

oopma

Serves **4**
Preparation time **10 minutes**
Cooking time **20 minutes**

175 g (6 oz) **coarse semolina**
3 tablespoons **vegetable oil**
1 teaspoon **black mustard seeds**
1 teaspoon **cumin seeds**
1 dried **red chilli**, chopped
10–12 **curry leaves**
1 **red onion**, finely chopped
1 **green chilli**, deseeded and chopped
50 g (2 oz) **raisins**
2 tablespoons **roasted cashew nuts**
50 g (2 oz) frozen **peas**
600 ml (1 pint) **hot water**
1 tablespoon **lemon juice**
2 tablespoons grated fresh **coconut**, plus extra to serve
2 tablespoons chopped fresh **coriander**
salt and **pepper**

Heat a large, heavy-based frying pan over a medium heat and dry-fry the semolina, stirring frequently, for 10 minutes or until it turns golden brown. Set aside.

Heat the oil in a large, nonstick frying pan and add the mustard and cumin seeds, dried chilli and curry leaves. Stir-fry for 30 seconds, then add the onion and fresh green chilli and continue to stir-fry until the onion has softened.

Add the raisins, cashew nuts, peas, semolina and measured hot water. Season and cook gently, stirring, until the semolina has absorbed all the water. Stir in the lemon juice, coconut and fresh coriander. Serve hot with natural yogurt, cucumber and grated coconut.

For oopma with chickpeas, use a drained 425 g (14 oz) can chickpeas instead of the peas and 100 g (3½ oz) Medjool dates, pitted and sliced, instead of the raisins. Proceed as above.

dhal makhani

Serves **4**

Preparation time **20 minutes**, plus soaking

Cooking time **about 1 hour**

125 g (4 oz) dried **split black lentils**

500 ml (17 fl oz) **boiling water**

3 tablespoons **butter**

1 **onion**, finely chopped

3 **garlic cloves**, crushed

2 teaspoons finely grated fresh **root ginger**

2 **green chillies**, split in half lengthways

1 teaspoon ground **turmeric**

1 teaspoon **paprika**, plus extra for sprinkling

1 tablespoon ground **cumin**

1 tablespoon ground **coriander**

200 g (7 oz) cooked or canned red **kidney beans**

500 ml (17 fl oz) **water**

200 g (7 oz) **baby leaf spinach**

salt

large handful of chopped fresh **coriander**

200 ml (7 fl oz) **single cream**

Place the black lentils in a sieve and wash under cold running water. Drain, place in a deep bowl and cover with cold water. Leave to soak for 10–12 hours.

Rinse the lentils then place in a saucepan with the measured boiling water. Bring to the boil, reduce the heat and simmer for 35–40 minutes or until tender. Drain and set aside.

Meanwhile, melt the butter in a large saucepan and add the onion, garlic, ginger and chillies. Stir-fry for 5–6 minutes and then add the turmeric, paprika, cumin, ground coriander, kidney beans and reserved lentils.

Add the measured water and bring the mixture to the boil. Reduce the heat and stir in the spinach. Cook gently for 10–15 minutes, stirring often. Remove from the heat and season with salt. Stir in the chopped fresh coriander and drizzle over the cream. Sprinkle over a little paprika and serve immediately in warmed bowls with hot Parathas (see page 226).

For dhal makhani with black beans, use a drained 425 g (14 oz) can black beans instead of the kidney beans and replace the baby leaf spinach with 150 g (5 oz) cabbage, finely shredded. Proceed as above.

cabbage bhaji

Serves **4**
Preparation time **10 minutes**
Cooking time **10 minutes**

500 g (1 lb) **white cabbage**,
roughly chopped
150 ml (¼ pint) **boiling water**
1 tablespoon **vegetable oil**
2 teaspoons **urad dhal** (dried
lentils)
1 teaspoon **black mustard
seeds**
1 dried **red chilli**, finely
chopped
6–8 **curry leaves**
2 tablespoons grated fresh
coconut
salt and **pepper**

Put the cabbage into a large saucepan with the water,
cover and cook over a medium heat for 10 minutes,
stirring occasionally. Drain, return to the pan, set aside
and keep warm.

Meanwhile, heat the oil in a small nonstick frying pan
and add the urad dhal, mustard seeds and chilli. Stir-
fry for 1–2 minutes and when the dhal turns light
brown add the curry leaves. Fry, stirring constantly,
for 2 minutes.

Pour the spiced oil over the cabbage, stir in the
coconut, season with salt and pepper and serve hot.

For mild-spiced cabbage bhaji, heat a small
saucepan, then add 1–2 tablespoons vegetable oil.
When hot add 1 tablespoon cumin seeds, 2 garlic
cloves, thinly sliced, and 1 teaspoon chopped ginger.
Stir-fry for 1–2 minutes, then pour the oil over the
prepared cabbage, as above. Season and serve hot.

baby aubergines with chilli

Serves **4**
Preparation time **20 minutes**
Cooking time **25–30 minutes**

500 g (1 lb) **baby aubergines**
5 tablespoons **sunflower oil**
6 **garlic cloves**, finely
  chopped
1 tablespoon finely chopped
  fresh **root ginger**
8 **spring onions**, cut
  diagonally into 2.5 cm
  (1 inch) lengths
2 **red chillies**, deseeded and
  finely sliced
3 tablespoons **light soy
  sauce**
1 tablespoon **Chinese rice
  wine**
1 tablespoon **palm sugar**
small handful of **mint** leaves
small handful of roughly
  chopped fresh **coriander**
100 g (3½ oz) canned **water
  chestnuts**, roughly chopped
50 g (2 oz) **roasted peanuts**,
  roughly chopped

Cut the aubergines in half lengthways and place on a heatproof plate. Place a trivet or steamer rack in a wok and pour in about 5 cm (2 inches) of water. Bring the water to the boil and lower the aubergine plate on to the trivet or rack.

Reduce the heat, cover and steam for 25–30 minutes (replenishing the water in the wok if needed) until the aubergines are cooked through and soft to the touch. Remove the aubergines from the wok, transfer to a serving platter and allow to cool.

Meanwhile, heat the oil in a nonstick frying pan. Add the garlic, ginger, spring onions and chillies and stir-fry for 2–3 minutes. Remove from the heat and stir in the soy sauce, rice wine and sugar.

Toss the mint leaves, coriander and water chestnuts with the aubergines and pour the garlic and ginger mixture evenly over the top. Sprinkle over the peanuts, toss gently and serve immediately with lime wedges and steamed egg noodles or rice, if liked.

For aubergine with bamboo shoots, use 2 large aubergines instead of the baby one. Dice them into 2 x 2 cm (⅞ x ⅞ inch) thick cubes and proceed as above. Add 50 g (2 oz) fresh red radishes, thinly sliced, and 100 g (3½ oz) canned bamboo shoots, drained, instead of water chestnuts.

spiced beetroot

Serves **4**
Preparation time **10 minutes**
Cooking time **5–6 minutes**

1 tablespoon **vegetable oil**
2 **garlic cloves**, finely
   chopped
1 teaspoon grated fresh **root
   ginger**
1 teaspoon **cumin seeds**
1 teaspoon **coriander seeds**,
   crushed
½ teaspoon dried red **chilli
   flakes**
625 g (1¼ lb) freshly cooked
   and peeled **beetroot**, cut
   into wedges
150 ml (¼ pint) **coconut milk**
¼ teaspoon ground
   cardamom seeds
grated rind and juice of
   1 **lime**
handful of chopped fresh
   coriander
salt and **pepper**

Heat the oil in a large frying pan and add the garlic, ginger, cumin, coriander seeds and chilli flakes. Stir-fry for 1–2 minutes, then add the beetroot. Fry, stirring gently, for 1 minute, then add the coconut milk, cardamom and lime rind and juice. Cook over a medium heat for 2–3 minutes.

Stir in the fresh coriander, season with salt and pepper and serve hot, warm or at room temperature.

For spiced mixed vegetables, replace the beetroot with 250 g (8 oz) cooked baby carrots (or chunks of large carrots), 250 g (8 oz) cooked swede, cut into cubes, and 250 g (8 oz) cooked parsnip, thickly sliced.

chickpea & spinach curry

Serves **4**

Preparation time **20 minutes**, plus soaking

Cooking time **about 1 hour**

200 g (7 oz) dried **chickpeas**

2 tablespoons **sunflower oil**

2 **onions**, thinly sliced

2 teaspoons ground **coriander**

2 teaspoons ground **cumin**

1 teaspoon hot **chilli powder**

½ teaspoon ground **turmeric**

1 tablespoon medium **curry powder**

400 g (13 oz) canned **chopped tomatoes**

1 teaspoon soft **brown sugar**

100 ml (3½ fl oz) **water**

2 tablespoons chopped **mint** leaves

100 g (3½ oz) **baby leaf spinach**

salt

natural yogurt, lightly whisked, to garnish (optional)

Soak the chickpeas in cold water overnight. Drain, rinse and place in a wok. Cover with water and bring to the boil. Reduce the heat and simmer for 45 minutes or until just tender. Drain and set aside.

Meanwhile, heat the oil in the wok, add the onions and cook over a low heat for 15 minutes until lightly golden. Add the coriander, cumin, chilli powder, turmeric and curry powder and stir-fry for 1–2 minutes.

Add the tomatoes, sugar and the measured water and bring to the boil. Cover, reduce the heat and simmer gently for 15 minutes.

Add the chickpeas, season well and cook gently for 8–10 minutes. Stir in the chopped mint. To serve, divide the spinach leaves between 4 shallow bowls and top with the chickpea mixture. Drizzle over some yogurt, if desired, and serve immediately with steamed rice or bread.

For curry filled baked sweet potato, scrub, prick and back 4 small sweet potatoes in a preheated oven at 200°C (400°F), Gas Mark 6 for about 1 hour, until tender. Split the sweet potatoes in half and fill with the curry. Top with yogurt or soured cream.

shallot & potato curry

Serves **4**
Preparation time **10 minutes**
Cooking time **18–20 minutes**

2 tablespoons **vegetable oil**
1 teaspoon coarsely ground
  coriander seeds
1 teaspoon **cumin seeds**
3 **plum tomatoes**, roughly
  chopped
10 **shallots**, peeled
1 teaspoon **chilli powder**
½ teaspoon ground **turmeric**
1 tablespoon **dhana-jeera**
1 teaspoon **sugar**
4–6 tablespoons **lemon juice**
3 large **potatoes**, cut into
  matchsticks
150 ml (¼ pint) **water**
2 tablespoons chopped fresh
  coriander
salt and **pepper**

Heat the oil in a large frying pan and add the ground coriander, cumin seeds, tomatoes and shallots. Stir-fry for 2 minutes, then add the chilli powder, turmeric, dhana-jeera, sugar and lemon juice to taste. Stir to mix well.

Add the potatoes and water, cover and cook gently for 10–15 minutes or until the potatoes are tender. Stir in the fresh coriander, season with salt and pepper and serve hot with pappadoms.

For spicy tortilla, use the curry in a slow-cooked tortilla. Beat 6 eggs in a large bowl and add the hot curry. Heat some sunflower oil in a large frying pan, pour in the mixture and cook gently for about 25–30 minutes, until almost set. Finish under a hot grill for 5–10 minutes, not too close to the heat, until browned on top and set. Leave to stand for 5 minutes. Serve in wedges.

creamy spiced mushrooms

Serves **4**
Preparation time **20 minutes**
Cooking time **15 minutes**

4 **garlic cloves,** finely
   chopped
2 teaspoons finely chopped
   fresh **root ginger**
1 **onion,** finely chopped
1 tablespoon mild **curry**
   powder
3 tablespoons **water**
5 tablespoons **sunflower oil**
500 g (1 lb) large **button**
   mushrooms, halved or
   thickly sliced
100 ml (3½ fl oz) **double**
   cream
2 tablespoons **tomato purée**
6 tablespoons finely chopped
   fresh **coriander**
salt and **pepper**

Place the garlic, ginger, onion and curry powder in a food processor with the measured water and blend until smooth.

Heat 3 tablespoons of the oil in a large nonstick wok or frying pan and add the mushrooms. Stir-fry over a high heat for 4–5 minutes. Transfer the mushrooms to a bowl and wipe the wok with kitchen paper.

Add the remaining oil to the wok and place over a medium heat. Add the onion mixture and stir-fry for 3–4 minutes. Add the mushrooms, cream and tomato purée and stir-fry for 3–4 minutes or until piping hot. Season well and remove from the heat. Serve immediately with flat bread. Garnished with chopped fresh coriander and freshly ground pepper.

For spiced mushroom pancakes, divide the spiced mushrooms among 8 ready-made pancakes and roll up. Place the pancakes in an ovenproof dish, dot with butter and spoon over an extra 125 ml (4 fl oz) cream. Cook in a preheated oven at 180°C (350°F), Gas Mark 4 for 15–20 minutes.

thai forest curry with lychees

Serves **4**

Preparation time **10 minutes**

Cooking time **8 minutes**

600 ml (1 pint) **water**

1 tablespoon **Thai red curry paste**

1 ¼ teaspoons **salt**

4 small round **aubergines**, quartered

50 g (2 oz) **green beans**, cut into 2.5 cm (1 inch) lengths

6 **lime leaves**, torn

20 g (¾ oz) **galangal** or fresh **root ginger**, unpeeled

4 **baby sweetcorn**

15 g (½ oz) **green peppercorns**

2 large **green chillies**

2 teaspoons **sugar**

20 fresh or canned **lychees**, peeled and stoned

20 g (¾ oz) **cucumber**, diced

Heat the measured water in a saucepan, add the curry paste and stir to blend thoroughly. Add the salt and bring to the boil, stirring occasionally.

Lower the heat to a slow boil and add all the other ingredients except the lychees and cucumber. Stir for 30 seconds.

Add the lychees and cucumber and cook, stirring occasionally, for 3–4 minutes. Serve in warmed bowls with steamed jasmine rice. Discard the piece of galangal or root ginger before serving.

For tofu & Thai forest curry, place 2 x 250 g (8 oz) blocks of tofu on a baking sheet. Brush with light soy sauce and drizzle with sunflower oil, then grill until brown. Turn the tofu over and brush with more soy sauce and drizzle over sunflower oil, then grill until brown. Slice the tofu and arrange on the curry.

bengali egg & potato curry

Serves **4**
Preparation time **30 minutes**
Cooking time **25–30 minutes**

2 tablespoons **sunflower oil**
1 tablespoon **black mustard seeds**
2 **garlic cloves**, crushed
2 dried **red chillies**
10 **curry leaves**
1 **onion**, thinly sliced
1 teaspoon **chilli powder**
1 tablespoon ground **coriander**
1 tablespoon **cumin seeds**
½ teaspoon ground **turmeric**
200 g (7 oz) canned **chopped tomatoes**
1 teaspoon **sugar**
400 ml (14 fl oz) **coconut milk**
6 **eggs**, hardboiled, shelled and halved lengthways
2 **potatoes**, boiled, peeled and cut into bite-sized pieces
salt
chopped **mint** leaves, to garnish

Heat the oil in a large nonstick wok or frying pan, then add the mustard seeds. When they start to pop, add the garlic, chillies and curry leaves and fry for 1 minute. Add the onion and cook, stirring constantly, for 5–6 minutes.

Stir in the chilli powder, ground coriander, cumin seeds and turmeric and then stir in the tomatoes and sugar. Bring to the boil, reduce the heat and simmer for 8–10 minutes, stirring often.

Stir in the coconut milk and add the eggs and potatoes. Cook gently for 8–10 minutes until the sauce has thickened. Season with salt and serve immediately, garnished with chopped mint leaves.

For Bengali prawn & egg curry, add 16 raw tiger prawns, peeled and deveined, to the curry about 6 minutes before the end of cooking and finish as above.

aubergine thai green curry

Serves **4**
Preparation time **7 minutes**
Cooking time **7–10 minutes**

300 ml (½ pint) **coconut milk**
40 g (1½ oz) **Thai green curry paste**
300 ml (½ pint) **vegetable stock**
4 small round **aubergines**, each cut into 8 pieces
40 g (1½ oz) **palm sugar**
1 teaspoon **salt**
4 teaspoons **vegetarian Thai fish sauce**
25 g (1 oz) **galangal** or fresh **root ginger**, peeled
425 g (14 oz) canned **straw mushrooms**, drained
50 g (2 oz) **green pepper**, thinly sliced

To garnish
handful of **Thai basil** leaves
2 tablespoons **coconut milk**

Heat the coconut milk in a saucepan with the curry paste, stirring to mix well. Add the stock and then the aubergines, sugar, salt, fish sauce, galangal or ginger and mushrooms.

Bring to the boil and cook, stirring, for 2 minutes. Add the green pepper, lower the heat and cook for 1 minute. Serve in a bowl, garnished with the basil leaves and drizzled with coconut milk. Discard the piece of galangal or root ginger before serving.

For bamboo shoot & water chestnut curry, omit the aubergines and replace with 125 g (4 oz) canned bamboo shoots and 125 g (4 oz) canned sliced water chestnuts. Add at the same time as the mushrooms. Reduce the quantity of stock to 150 ml (¼ pint).

thai pumpkin curry

Serves **4**

Preparation time **20 minutes**

Cooking time **40–45 minutes**

2 tablespoons **sunflower oil**

12 **Thai shallots**, peeled

2 **garlic cloves**, crushed

1 teaspoon finely grated fresh **root ginger**

3 tablespoons **Thai red curry paste**

750 g (1½ lb) **pumpkin**, peeled and cut into bite-sized pieces

400 ml (14 fl oz) **coconut milk**

150 ml (¼ pint) **vegetable stock**

6 **lime leaves**

2 teaspoons grated **palm sugar**

3 **lemon grass stalks**, bruised

300 g (10 oz) **sugarsnap peas**, trimmed

large handful of finely chopped fresh **coriander**

50 g (2 oz) roughly chopped **roasted peanuts**

salt

Heat the oil in a large nonstick wok or frying pan. Add the Thai shallots, garlic and ginger and stir-fry for 3–4 minutes. Stir in the curry paste and pumpkin and continue to stir-fry for 3–4 minutes.

Add the coconut milk, stock, lime leaves, palm sugar and lemon grass stalks. Bring to the boil, reduce the heat and simmer gently for 20–25 minutes, stirring occasionally.

Stir in the sugarsnap peas and cook for another 6–8 minutes or until the vegetables are just tender. Season with salt.

Remove from the heat and sprinkle over the fresh coriander and peanuts just before serving.

For pumpkin & chicken curry, prepare 400 g (13 oz) skinless chicken breast, cutting it into bite-sized chunks. Add to the curry with the onions and continue with the recipe as above.

paneer korma

Serves **4**
Preparation time **20 minutes**
Cooking time **about**
  30 minutes

2 tablespoons **sunflower oil**
8 **shallots**, finely chopped
1 teaspoon ground **cumin**
1 teaspoon ground **coriander**
1 teaspoon ground **turmeric**
1 teaspoon **chilli powder**
1 teaspoon **garam masala**
4 ripe **plum tomatoes**,
  roughly chopped
2 teaspoons crushed **garlic**
2 **red chillies**, deseeded and
  finely sliced
2 tablespoons **tomato purée**
1 teaspoon **sugar**
150 ml (¼ pint) **water**
200 ml (7 fl oz) **single cream**
450 g (14½ oz) **paneer**
  (Indian cheese), cut into bite-
  sized pieces
200 g (7 oz) frozen **peas**
finely chopped fresh
  coriander, to garnish
pappadoms, to serve

Heat the oil in a large nonstick wok or frying pan, add the shallots and stir-fry for 2–3 minutes. Add the ground spices and stir-fry for 1 minute.

Add the tomatoes, garlic, chillies, tomato purée, sugar and measured water and bring to the boil. Reduce the heat and simmer, uncovered, for 15–20 minutes.

Stir in the cream, paneer and peas and simmer gently for 5 minutes or until the paneer is heated through and the peas are cooked.

Season well, remove from the heat and stir in the chopped fresh coriander just before serving. Serve immediately with crisp pappadoms.

For royal paneer korma pilau, cook 250 g (8 oz) basmati rice according to the packet instructions. Add the rice to the cooked korma, forking the ingredients together carefully. Garnish with crispy fried onions, if liked.

thai yellow curry with carrots

Serves **4**

Preparation time **15 minutes**

Cooking time **35–40 minutes**

150 ml (¼ pint) **vegetable stock**

5 **lime leaves**, plus extra to garnish

25 g (1 oz) **galangal** or fresh **root ginger**, peeled and sliced

175 g (6 oz) **carrots**, cut into chunks

4 **garlic cloves**, crushed

2 large **red** or **green chillies**

1 tablespoon **groundnut oil**

2 tablespoons **roasted peanuts**, coarsely chopped

300 ml (½ pint) **coconut milk**

2 tablespoons **Thai yellow curry paste**

8 canned **straw mushrooms**, drained

4 **shallots**

salt

Put the vegetable stock in a saucepan, add the lime leaves, the galangal or ginger, carrots, half the crushed garlic and the chillies. Simmer for 15 minutes. Strain the stock, reserving the liquid and both the carrots and chillies separately.

Heat the oil in a saucepan and fry the remaining garlic for 1 minute. Add the reserved carrots and the peanuts and cook, stirring, for 1 minute. Add the coconut milk and curry paste and stir until well blended. Now add the reserved liquid, the mushrooms and shallots and simmer, stirring occasionally, for 15 minutes or until the shallots are cooked. Season to taste.

Deseed and finely slice the reserved cooked chillies. Use to garnish the curry.

For Thai yellow curry with butternut squash,
use 250 g (8 oz) peeled butternut squash, cut into chunks, instead of carrots. Prepare the curry as above.

curried tofu with vegetables

Serves **4**
Preparation time **20 minutes**
Cooking time **25 minutes**

2 tablespoons **sunflower oil**
2 teaspoons finely grated
  fresh **root ginger**
8 **garlic cloves**, chopped
8 small **shallots**, chopped
1 teaspoon ground **turmeric**
2 **red chillies**, chopped
4 tablespoons very finely
  chopped **lemon grass**
400 ml (14 fl oz) **coconut
  milk**
200 ml (7 fl oz) **vegetable
  stock**
4 **lime leaves**, finely shredded
12 **baby courgettes**, cut in
  half lengthways
12 **baby sweetcorn**, trimmed
  and cut in half lengthways
400 g (13 oz) **firm tofu**, cut
  into bite-sized cubes
1 tablespoon **dark soy sauce**
1 tablespoon **lime juice**
salt and **pepper**
small handful of roughly
  chopped fresh **coriander**
finely chopped **red chillies**

Place the oil, ginger, garlic, shallots, turmeric, chillies, lemon grass and half the coconut milk in a food processor and process until fairly smooth.

Heat a large nonstick wok and pour the coconut mixture into it. Stir-fry over a high heat for 3–4 minutes and then add the remaining coconut milk, the stock and lime leaves. Bring to the boil, reduce the heat and simmer gently, uncovered, for 10 minutes.

Add the courgettes and baby sweetcorn to the mixture and simmer for 6–7 minutes. Stir in the tofu, soy sauce and lime juice, season to taste and cook gently for 1–2 minutes.

Remove from the heat and stir in the fresh coriander. Serve in bowls garnished with basil leaves.

For pattypan curry with tofu or seafood, replace the baby courgettes and sweetcorn with pattypan squash. Cook as above. For seafood-lovers, replace the tofu with 16–20 raw tiger prawns and 500 g (1 lb) squid rings. Add the prawns and squid to the curry with the vegetables and finish as above.

tarka dhal

Serves **4**
Preparation time **10 minutes**,
  plus soaking
Cooking time **25 minutes**

250 g (8 oz) **red split lentils**
1 litre (1½ pints) **hot water**
200 g (7 oz) canned **chopped tomatoes**
2 **green chillies**, deseeded and finely chopped (optional)
¼ teaspoon ground **turmeric**
2 teaspoons grated fresh **root ginger**
4 tablespoons chopped fresh **coriander**
salt and **pepper**

Tarka
1 tablespoon **sunflower oil**
2 teaspoons **black mustard seeds**
1 teaspoon **cumin seeds**
2 **garlic cloves**, thinly sliced
1 dried **red chilli**

Soak the lentils in boiling water to cover for 10 minutes. Drain and put into a large saucepan with the measured hot water. Bring to the boil over a high heat, spooning off any scum that comes to the surface. Reduce the heat and cook for 20 minutes or until soft and tender.

Drain the lentils and process to a purée in a food processor or using a hand-held electric whisk. Return the purée to the rinsed pan with the tomatoes, chillies (if using), turmeric, ginger and fresh coriander. Season with salt and pepper, return to the heat and simmer gently for 5 minutes.

Meanwhile, make the tarka. Heat the oil in a small nonstick frying pan and add the remaining ingredients. Fry, stirring constantly, for 1–2 minutes.

Remove the tarka from the heat and pour on to the cooked dhal. Stir and serve hot with basmati rice, natural yogurt, if liked, Naan (see page 224) and Lime Pickle (see page 234).

For tarka dhal with yellow lentils & spinach, use 250 g (8 oz) yellow split lentils instead of red lentils. Make in the same way as above, but cook the soaked and drained lentils with 250 g (8 oz) finely chopped baby leaf spinach.

cumin potatoes

Serves **4**
Preparation time **20 minutes**
Cooking time **5–7 minutes**

4 tablespoons **sunflower oil**
1 teaspoon **black mustard seeds**
3 teaspoons **cumin seeds**
8–10 **curry leaves**
2 teaspoons ground **cumin**
2 teaspoons ground **coriander**
1 teaspoon ground **turmeric**
500 g (1 lb) **potatoes**, cooked, peeled and cut into 2.5 cm (1 inch) cubes
4 tablespoons chopped fresh **coriander**
lime juice, for squeezing
salt

Heat the oil in a large nonstick wok or frying pan. Add the mustard seeds, cumin seeds and curry leaves.

Stir-fry for 1–2 minutes and then add the ground spices and potatoes. Season well and stir-fry over a high heat for 4–5 minutes.

Remove from the heat, stir in the fresh coriander and squeeze in lime juice to taste.

For spicy potato tortilla wraps, heat 8 tortillas following the instructions on the packet and roughly shred half an iceberg lettuce. Divide the cumin potatoes among the tortillas and top with some lettuce. Drizzle with 75 g (3 oz) yogurt, lightly whisked, and roll up.

on the side

spiced rice with lentils

Serves **4**

Preparation time **20 minutes,**
  plus standing

Cooking time **20–25 minutes**

125 g (4 oz) **red split lentils**
225 g (7½ oz) **basmati rice**
3 tablespoons **sunflower oil**
1 **onion,** finely chopped
1 teaspoon ground **turmeric**
1 tablespoon **cumin seeds**
1 dried **red chilli**
1 **cinnamon stick**
3 **cloves**
3 **cardamom pods,** lightly
  bruised
500 ml (17 fl oz) **vegetable
  stock**
8 **cherry tomatoes,** halved
6 tablespoons finely chopped
  fresh **coriander**
salt and **pepper**
crispy fried **onions,** to garnish

Wash the lentils and rice several times in cold water.
Drain thoroughly.

Heat the oil in a heavy-based saucepan and add the
onion. Stir-fry for 6–8 minutes over a medium heat
and then add the spices.

Continue to stir-fry for 2–3 minutes, then add the
rice and lentils. Stir-fry for another 2–3 minutes, then
add the stock, tomatoes and fresh coriander. Season
well and bring to the boil. Reduce the heat, cover
tightly and simmer for 10 minutes.

Remove the pan from the heat and allow to stand
undisturbed for another 10 minutes. Transfer to a
serving dish and garnish with crispy fried onions.
Serve immediately with pickles and natural yogurt,
if liked.

For spiced rice with yellow split peas, use the
same quantity of yellow split peas instead of red
lentils – they can be treated in exactly the same way.
Proceed as above.

fragrant coconut rice

Serves **4**

Preparation time **5 minutes**,
  plus soaking and standing

Cooking time **15 minutes**

225 g (7½ oz) **basmati rice**

2 tablespoons **vegetable oil**

2 teaspoons black **mustard seeds**

1 teaspoon **cumin seeds**

10 **curry leaves**

1 dried red **chilli**, finely chopped

100 ml (3½ fl oz) **coconut milk**

375 ml (13 fl oz) **boiling water**

salt and **pepper**

roasted **cashew nuts**, to garnish

Wash the rice several times in cold water, then leave to soak for 15 minutes. Drain thoroughly.

Heat the oil in a large heavy-based saucepan and add the mustard and cumin seeds, curry leaves and dried chilli. Add the rice to the pan and stir-fry for 1–2 minutes. Add the coconut milk and boiling water, season with salt and pepper and then bring back to the boil.

Cover tightly, reduce the heat and simmer gently for 10–12 minutes. Do not lift the lid, as the steam is required for the cooking process.

Remove the pan from the heat and leave to stand, covered and undisturbed, for 8–10 minutes. To serve, fluff up the grains of rice with a fork and garnish with roasted cashew nuts. Serve as an accompaniment to fish or seafood dishes.

For fragrant coconut rice with fresh coconut, use 100 g (3½ oz) finely grated fresh coconut. Add to the rice with the boiling water, increasing the amount of water to 450 ml (¾ pint). Proceed as above.

vegetable fried rice

Serves **4**
Preparation time **20 minutes**
Cooking time **12—15 minutes**

2 tablespoons **sunflower oil**
2 **garlic cloves**, finely
   chopped
4 **red shallots**, thinly sliced
1 small **red chilli**, finely sliced
100 g (3½ oz) **carrots**, cut into
   thin matchsticks
100 g (3½ oz) **fine green
   beans**, cut into 2.5 cm
   (1 inch) lengths
100 g (3½ oz) fresh
   sweetcorn kernels
1 **red pepper**, deseeded and
   cut into 1 cm (½ inch) dice
100 g (3½ oz) **shitake
   mushrooms**, thinly sliced
500 g (1 lb) cooked, cooled
   long-grain rice
3 tablespoons **light soy sauce**
2 teaspoons **Thai green curry
   paste**
lime wedges, for squeezing
   (optional)

Heat a wok over a high heat and add the garlic,
shallots and chilli. Stir-fry for 1—2 minutes and then
add the carrots, green beans, sweetcorn, red pepper
and mushrooms. Stir-fry for 3—4 minutes.

Add the rice and stir-fry for 4—5 minutes. Mix together
the soy sauce and curry paste and add to the wok.
Toss to mix well and stir-fry for 2—3 minutes until
piping hot. Serve with wedges of lime for squeezing,
if liked.

For fried rice with prawns & egg, use 200 g (7 oz)
cooked peeled prawns and add them to the dish
when you add the rice. Just before serving, top each
portion with an egg, fried over a high heat so the white
is crisp around the edges but the yolk is still runny.

saffron & cardamom rice

Serves **4**

Preparation time **15 minutes**,
  plus soaking and standing

Cooking time **about
  15 minutes**

225 g (7½ oz) **basmati rice**

15 g (½ oz) **unsalted butter**

1 tablespoon **vegetable oil**

1 **onion**, finely chopped

2 dried **red chillies**

6 **cardamom pods**, lightly
  crushed

1 **cinnamon stick**

1 teaspoon **cumin seeds**

2 **bay leaves**

1 teaspoon **saffron threads**,
  soaked in 1 tablespoon **hot
  milk**

475 ml (16 fl oz) **boiling
  water**

salt and **pepper**

Wash the rice several times in cold water, then leave to soak for 15 minutes. Drain thoroughly.

Heat the butter and oil in a large heavy-based saucepan and add the onion. Stir and cook over a medium heat for 2–3 minutes. Add the chillies, cardamom, cinnamon, cumin and bay leaves.

Add the rice to the pan and stir-fry for 2–3 minutes. Then add the saffron mixture and boiling water, season with salt and pepper and bring back to the boil. Cover tightly, reduce the heat and simmer gently for 10 minutes. Do not lift the lid, as the steam is required for the cooking process.

Remove the pan from the heat and leave the rice to stand, covered and undisturbed, for 8–10 minutes. Fluff up the grains with a fork and serve immediately.

For smoked salmon kedgeree, add 200 g (7 oz) shredded smoked salmon and 4 roughly chopped hard-boiled eggs to the cooked saffron rice.

nasi goreng

Serves **4**
Preparation time **25 minutes**
Cooking time **15 minutes**

2 tablespoons **sunflower oil**
2 **eggs**, lightly beaten with
 ¼ teaspoon ground **turmeric**
1 **onion**, thinly sliced
6 **spring onions**, cut
 diagonally into 2.5 cm
 (1 inch) lengths
2 **garlic cloves**, crushed
1 teaspoon finely grated fresh
 root ginger
100 g (3½ oz) **Chinese
 cabbage**, finely shredded
1 **red pepper**, deseeded and
 thinly sliced
50 g (2 oz) **bean sprouts**
750 g (1½ lb) cooked, cooled
 long-grain rice
1 tablespoon **kecap manis**
1 tablespoon **sambal oelek**
chopped fresh **coriander**
 and **mint leaves**, to garnish

Heat ½ tablespoon of the oil in a nonstick frying pan.
Add half the egg mixture and swirl the pan to make
a thin omelette. When set, remove from the pan, roll
up and cut into thin strips.

Repeat with another ½ tablespoon of the oil and the
remaining egg mixture. Set aside.

Heat the remaining oil in a large nonstick wok and
add the onion, spring onions, garlic and ginger.
Stir-fry for 4—5 minutes, then add the cabbage, red
pepper and bean sprouts. Stir-fry over a high heat for
3—4 minutes.

Stir in the cooked rice, kecap manis, sambal oelek
and the omelette strips. Stir-fry for 3—4 minutes or
until the rice is heated through and piping hot.

Remove from the heat and serve immediately,
garnished with the chopped herbs.

For nasi goreng with chicken, add about 200 g
(7 oz) shredded cooked chicken to the wok with the
rice and make sure all the ingredients are piping hot
before serving.

tamarind rice

Serves **4**
Preparation time **10 minutes**
Cooking time **about
20 minutes**

1 tablespoon **sunflower oil**
1 large **red onion**, thinly sliced
2 **aubergines** cut into cubes
1 **red chilli**, deseeded and
   thinly sliced
2 tablespoons **tamarind
   paste**
1 tablespoon dark
   muscovado sugar
500 g (1 lb) cooked **basmati
   rice**
8 tablespoons fresh **mint**
   leaves, roughly chopped
200 g (7 oz) **baby spinach
   leaves**
salt and **pepper**

Warm the oil in a large frying pan over a medium heat.
Add the sliced onion and cook for 10 minutes or until
lightly browned.

Increase the heat to high. Add the cubed aubergine,
half of the sliced chilli, a tablespoon of tamarind and
the muscovado sugar. Stir-fry for 5 minutes until the
aubergine is golden and beginning to soften.

Add the cooked rice, mint, spinach and the remaining
tamarind to the aubergine and onion mixture. Continue
to stir-fry for 5–6 minutes or until piping hot.

Sprinkle over the remaining chilli slices. Season with
salt and pepper and serve immediately.

For tamarind & dill rice, replace the aubergines with
2 finely diced courgettes and use 8 tablespoons
finely chopped fresh dill, instead of the mint. Proceed
as above, omitting the chilli slices.

tomato & fennel rice

Serves **4**
Preparation time **20 minutes**,
  plus soaking and standing
Cooking time **about
  20 minutes**

275 g (9 oz) **basmati rice**
3 tablespoons **sunflower oil**
4 **shallots**, finely chopped
2 teaspoons **fennel seeds**
2 **garlic cloves**, finely
  chopped
4 ripe **tomatoes**, skinned,
  deseeded and finely
  chopped
500 ml (17 fl oz) **hot water**
2 tablespoons finely chopped
  fresh **coriander**
salt and **pepper**

Wash the rice several times in cold water, then leave
to soak for 15 minutes. Drain thoroughly.

Heat the oil in a heavy-based saucepan and fry the
shallots, fennel and garlic for 4–5 minutes. Add
the tomatoes and rice and stir-fry for 2–3 minutes.
Season well and pour over the measured hot water.
Cover tightly, reduce the heat and simmer gently for
10 minutes. Do not lift the lid, as the steam is required
for the cooking process.

Remove the pan from the heat and leave the rice to
stand, covered and undisturbed, for 8–10 minutes.
Fluff up the grains with a fork, stir in the fresh
coriander and serve immediately.

For cherry tomato & almond rice, replace the fennel
seeds with an equal quantity of coarsely crushed
coriander seeds and use 250 g (8 oz) halved cherry
tomatoes instead of diced tomatoes. When you fluff up
the rice, add 2 tablespoons toasted flaked almonds.

fragrant persian herbed rice

Serves **4**

Preparation time **20 minutes,**
 plus soaking

Cooking time **30–35 minutes**

425 g (14 oz) **basmati rice**

50 g (2 oz) **butter**, plus extra
 to serve (optional)

75 ml (3 fl oz) **sunflower oil**

1 **cinnamon stick**

2 **cardamom pods**, lightly
 crushed

2 **cloves**

100 g (3½ oz) mixture of fresh
 dill, **coriander** and **mint**,
 roughly chopped

salt and **pepper**

Wash the rice well until the water runs clear. Put the rice in a bowl, cover with water and leave to soak for 2 hours. Wash again.

Bring a saucepan of water to the boil, then add the rice. Cook the rice for about 6 minutes until it begins to soften on the outside. Drain and rinse in lukewarm water.

Heat the butter and oil in a heavy saucepan until foaming, then add the spices and half of the rice. Cover the rice with half the herbs. Add the remaining rice then finish with the remaining herbs. Season each layer with salt and pepper.

Turn the heat down to low and make 3 steam holes in the rice with the handle of a wooden spoon. Wrap the lid of the saucepan in a clean tea towel and place it on the saucepan – the tea towel stops condensation from falling into the rice. Leave the rice to cook for 20–25 minutes.

Empty the rice into a bowl. Scrap off and break up the lovely crisp bits at the bottom of the saucepan and add them to the rice. Add additional butter, if liked. Serve immediately with a curry of your choice.

For quick Persian herbed rice, stir-fry pre-prepared cooked and cooled rice in a large wok or frying pan with 2 tablespoons of butter, 2 cloves, 1 cinnamon stick and 2 crushed cardamom pods. When piping hot, add the chopped fresh herbs. Stir-fry for a further 2–3 minutes. Season well before serving.

carrot & pea pilaf

Serves **4**
Preparation time **20 minutes**,
  plus soaking and standing
Cooking time **14–16 minutes**

275 g (9 oz) **basmati rice**
4 tablespoons **sunflower oil**
1 **cinnamon stick**
2 teaspoons **cumin seeds**
2 **cloves**
4 **cardamom pods**, lightly
  bruised
8 black **peppercorns**
1 large **carrot**, peeled and
  coarsely grated
200 g (7 oz) frozen **peas**
500 ml (17 fl oz) **hot water**
salt and **pepper**

Wash the rice several times in cold water, then leave to soak for 15 minutes. Drain thoroughly.

Heat the oil in a heavy-based saucepan and add the spices. Stir-fry for 2–3 minutes and then add the carrot and peas. Stir-fry for 2–3 minutes and then add the rice. Stir and pour in the measured hot water. Season well.

Bring to the boil, cover tightly, reduce the heat and simmer gently for 10 minutes. Do not lift the lid, as the steam is required for the cooking process.

Remove the pan from the heat and leave the rice to stand, covered and undisturbed, for 8–10 minutes. Fluff up the grains with a fork and serve immediately.

For prawn & egg pilaf, stir in 300 g (10 oz) cooked peeled prawns when you add the rice to the pan. Just before serving, add 2 chopped hard-boiled eggs and a handful of chopped coriander. Stir through.

roti

Makes **8**
Preparation time **20 minutes**,
  plus resting
Cooking time **about**
  15 minutes

100 g (3½ oz) **wholemeal
  flour**
100 g (3½ oz) **gram flour**
  (besan)
2 tablespoons finely chopped
  coriander leaves
1 **red chilli**, finely chopped
2 teaspoons ground **cumin**
1 teaspoon ground **turmeric**
1 teaspoon **salt**
6 tablespoons melted **butter**
  or **ghee**, plus extra for
  brushing
200 ml (7 fl oz) **water**

Sift the flours into a large mixing bowl and add the
remaining ingredients except the water. Mix together
and gradually add the measured water to form a soft,
pliable dough.

Knead on a lightly floured surface for 1–2 minutes,
then cover and allow to rest for 10 minutes.

Divide the mixture into 8 balls and roll each one out
into a 12–15 cm (5–6 inch) disc. Brush the top of
each one with a little melted butter or ghee.

Heat a nonstick griddle or frying pan over a high heat
and, when hot, cook the breads, one at a time, for
35–40 seconds on each side, pressing down with a
spatula for even cooking.

Remove each roti from the heat and keep warm,
wrapped in foil, while cooking the remaining breads.
Serve warm with any curry of your choice.

For onion roti, add ½ onion, very finely chopped, to
the dough. Remove the seeds from the chilli if you
want a milder bread.

naan

Makes **8**
Preparation time **20 minutes**,
  plus resting
Cooking time **about
  20 minutes**

450 g (14½ oz) **self-raising
  flour**
2 teaspoons **sugar**
1 teaspoon **salt**
1 teaspoon **baking powder**
4 tablespoons melted **butter**
  or **ghee**, plus extra for
  brushing
250 ml (8 fl oz) **warm milk**
2 tablespoons **nigella seeds**

Sift the flour, sugar, salt and baking powder in a large mixing bowl. Add the melted butter or ghee and rub into the flour mixture with your fingers. Gradually add the warm milk and mix to a soft dough.

Transfer to a lightly floured surface and knead for 6–8 minutes or until smooth. Place in the bowl, cover with clingfilm and set aside for 20–25 minutes.

Divide the mixture into 8 portions and flatten each one into a thick cake. Cover with a cloth and set aside for 10–15 minutes.

Roll each piece into a disc about 23 cm (9 inches) in diameter. Brush the tops of the breads with butter or ghee and sprinkle over the nigella seeds.

Place the breads on a lightly oiled grill rack and cook in batches under a preheated medium-high grill for 1–2 minutes on each side, or until puffed up and lightly browned in spots. Wrap in a clean tea towel while you finish cooking the rest.

Serve warm with any curry of your choice.

For fragrant naan, you can add a variety of ingredients in the first step when you make the dough. For garlic-flavoured naan, add 1 garlic clove, finely chopped. For coriander-flavoured naan, add 4 tablespoons fresh coriander, roughly chopped. For cumin-flavoured naan, add 1 tablespoon cumin seeds.

paratha

Makes **12**
Preparation time **20 minutes**,
  plus resting
Cooking time **24 minutes**

225 g (7½ oz) **wholemeal
  flour**, plus extra for dusting
100 g (3½ oz) **plain flour**
1 teaspoon ground
  cardamom
2 teaspoons **salt**
250 g (8 oz) warm **buttermilk**
125 ml (4 fl oz) **sunflower oil**

Sift the flours into a large mixing bowl and add the cardamom and salt. Work in the buttermilk and 1 tablespoon of the oil to make a soft dough.

Knead on a lightly floured surface for 10 minutes and form into a ball. Cover with a damp cloth and leave to rest for 20 minutes.

Divide the dough into 12 balls and roll each one out into a 15 cm (6 inch) disc. Brush a paratha with a little oil, fold in half and then brush again. Fold in half again to form a triangle, dust with a little flour and flatten with a rolling pin to make a 15 cm (6 inch) triangle. Repeat with the remaining breads.

Heat a nonstick griddle pan or frying pan over a medium heat. Brush with a little oil and cook each paratha for 1 minute, pressing down with a spatula. Turn it over, brush with a little more oil and cook for a further 1 minute.

Remove each paratha and keep warm wrapped in foil while you cook the remaining breads. Serve warm with any curry of your choice.

For garlic parathas, add 2 cloves of garlic, crushed, in the first step when you make the dough.

bhatura

Makes **10**
Preparation time **10 minutes**,
  plus resting
Cooking time **10 minutes**

175 g (6 oz) **self-raising
  flour**, plus extra for dusting
1 tablespoon **sunflower oil**
1 tablespoon **natural yogurt**
1 teaspoon **salt**
2–3 tablespoons **water**
oil, for deep-frying

Mix the flour, oil, yogurt and salt in a large mixing bowl and add enough water to make a soft dough. Cover the bowl with a clean tea towel and leave to rest for 15 minutes.

Turn the dough out on to a lightly floured surface and knead well for 3–4 minutes or until smooth. Divide the mixture into 10 portions and roll each portion into a ball. Roll each ball into a 7 cm (3 inch) disc and set aside to rest.

Pour the oil for deep-frying into a wok or large frying pan until one-third full and heat to 180–190°C (350–375°F), or until a cube of bread browns in 30 seconds.

Slide 2–3 bhaturas into the pan. When the bhaturas puff up, turn them over and fry for 1 minute more or until lightly browned on both sides. Carefully remove with a slotted spoon and drain on kitchen paper.

Repeat with the remaining bhaturas and serve immediately.

For extra rich bhatura, use butter or ghee in the mixture instead of the oil. Use 15 g (½ oz) butter or ghee and rub it into the flour and salt before stirring in the yogurt. Finish as above.

tamarind & date chutney

Serves **4**

Preparation time **10 minutes**

200 g (7 oz) stoned **dried
   dates**, roughly chopped
1 tablespoon **tamarind paste**
1 teaspoon ground **cumin**
1 teaspoon **chilli powder**
1 tablespoon **tomato ketchup**
200 ml (7 fl oz) **water**
salt

Put all the ingredients into a food processor or blender and process until fairly smooth.

Transfer the mixture to a serving bowl, cover and chill until required. The chutney will keep for up to 3 days in the refrigerator.

For chutney-marinated paneer, spoon the chutney over 250 g (8 oz) paneer, cubed, and leave to marinate for several hours. Drain well. Cover the grill shelf with foil and brush with oil. Spread out the paneer on the foil and cook under a preheated hot grill until browned, turning as necessary.

mango, apple & mint chutney

Serves **4–6**
Preparation time **10 minutes**

1 **green mango,** peeled,
  stoned and roughly chopped
1 small **apple**, peeled, cored
  and roughly chopped
1 teaspoon **salt**
1 tablespoon chopped **mint**
  leaves
1 teaspoon mild **chilli powder**
1 teaspoon soft **brown sugar**
150 ml (¼ pint) **water**

Put all the ingredients into a food processor or blender and process until smooth.

Transfer the mixture to a small serving dish, cover and chill until required. The chutney will keep for up to 3 days in the refrigerator.

For mango & peach chutney, replace the apple with 1–2 ripe peaches, stoned and chopped. Add a squeeze of lime juice to counteract the sweetness. Pear is also a good substitute for the apple.

lime pickle

Makes **1 jar**
Preparation time **20 minutes**,
  plus maturing
Cooking time **5 minutes**

10 **limes**, each cut into
  6 segments
100 g (3½ oz) **salt**
1 tablespoon **fenugreek**
  seeds
1 tablespoon **black mustard**
  seeds
1 tablespoon **chilli powder**
1 tablespoon ground **turmeric**
300 ml (½ pint) **vegetable oil**
½ teaspoon **asafoetida**

Put the limes into a sterilized jar and cover with the salt. Dry-fry the fenugreek and mustard seeds in a small frying pan, and then grind them to a powder. Add the ground seeds, chilli powder and turmeric to the limes and mix well.

Heat the oil in a small frying pan until smoking, add the asafoetida and fry for 30 seconds. Pour the oil over the limes and mix well.

Cover the jar with a clean cloth and leave to mature for 10 days in a bright, warm place.

Transfer the pickle to a tightly covered container and store for up to 2 months.

For carrot & lime pickle, use 5 limes and 1 large carrot peeled and cut into 1.5 cm (½ inch) pieces. Proceed as above.

index

238

acknowledgements

Executive Editor: Nicky Hill
Editor: Camilla Davis
Executive Designer: Darren Southern
Designer: Martin Topping 'ome Design
Photographer: Stephen Conroy
Home Economist: Sunil Vijayakar
Food and Props Stylist: Liz Hippisley
Production Manager: Nigel Reed

Special photography: © Octopus Publishing
  Group Ltd/Stephen Conroy.
Other photography: © Octopus Publishing Group
  Ltd/David Loftus 60; /Lis Parsons 65; /Neil
  Marsh 159; /Sandra Lane 194; /William Reavell
  19, 20, 27, 33, 33, 87, 95, 137, 141, 145, 169,
  173, 180, 199, 207, 228.